Ross, Christina.
Love fed

"*Love Fed* is a must ~~~ addiction (like myself!) looking to ~~~ sserts for vegan guilt-free superfood ~~~ good for your body."

— ...rO, health and wellness expert,
bestselling author, and champion athlete

"I've always believed that raw vegan desserts are the perfect gateway to a healthier lifestyle. Lucky for all of us, *Love Fed* provides the perfect caramel-covered bridge to the promised land! Christina's decadent desserts are simple enough for novice chefs to prepare at home and full of nutritious superfoods that hardcore health foodies will swoon over. From tantalizing truffles to insane ice creams and perfect pies (oh my), I'm still wiping my drool off the pages. I can't think of a more beautiful and accessible book to help you take the guilt out of your everyday dessert pleasures!"

—JASON WROBEL, celebrity vegan chef
and host of *How to Live to 100* on
Cooking Channel

"Forget 'sinful' treats without nutritional benefits. Nourish yourself with love. Christina's creations are as healthful as they are divine."

—MATTHEW KENNEY, chef, author,
and entrepreneur

"As an unapologetic omnivore in the tradition of Anthony Bourdain and Andrew Zimmern, I must admit, *Love Fed* did inspire drool production in my mouth, especially the Banana-Toffee Pie recipe. I suppose that makes this book drool-worthy!"

—EDDIE LIN, author of *Extreme Cuisine*
and blogger for Deep End Dining

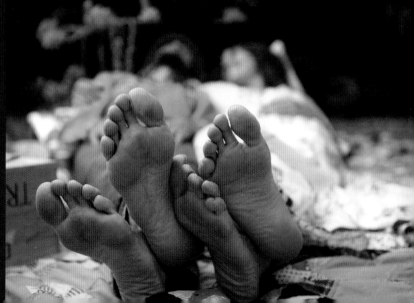

LOVE FED

Purely Decadent, Simply Raw, Plant-Based Desserts

CHRISTINA ROSS

BenBella

BENBELLA BOOKS, INC.
DALLAS, TEXAS

Copyright © 2015 by Christina Ross

All rights reserved. No part of this book may be used or reproduced in any manner whatsoever without written permission except in the case of brief quotations embodied in critical articles or reviews.

BenBella Books, Inc.
10300 N. Central Expressway
Suite #530
Dallas, TX 75231
www.benbellabooks.com
Send feedback to feedback@benbellabooks.com

Printed in the United States of America
10 9 8 7 6 5 4 3 2 1

Library of Congress Cataloging-in-Publication Data
Ross, Christina.
    Love fed : purely decadent, simply raw, plant-based desserts / by Christina Ross.
       pages cm
    Includes bibliographical references and index.
    ISBN 978-1-940363-32-5 (paperback)—ISBN 978-1-940363-49-3 (electronic) 1. Desserts. 2. Vegetarian cooking. 3. Raw foods I. Title.
    TX773.R7946 2015
    641.86—dc23

                                                                      2014028385

Editing by Heather Butterfield
Copyediting by Karen Levy
Proofreading by James Fraleigh and Kristin Vorce
Indexing by WordCo Indexing Services
Photography by Christina Ross unless otherwise indicated.
Photography on pages iv (bottom right), viii (middle left), xvi–xviii, 3–4, 85, 94, 97, 110, 115, 121, 131, 179, 199, 217, 226, and 236 by Christiane Ingenthron
Photography on pages iv (top middle), xv, 10, 15, 26, 40, 107, 144, 150, 207, and 224 by Alex Thevenot
Cover design, text design, and composition by Kris Tobiassen of Matchbook Digital
Printed by Versa Press

Distributed by Perseus Distribution
www.perseusdistribution.com

To place orders through Perseus Distribution:
Tel: (800) 343-4499
Fax: (800) 351-5073
E-mail: orderentry@perseusbooks.com

Significant discounts for bulk sales are available. Please contact Glenn Yeffeth at glenn@benbellabooks.com or (214) 750-3628.

To Alex and Nova

Your love feeds me ever so sweetly.
I am blessed and grateful to call you my beloveds!
It is because of your love and encouragement to follow my heart
that this book was birthed.

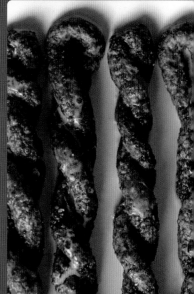

CONTENTS

ACKNOWLEDGMENTS

If it weren't for love and inspiration a book such as this would not exist, so it is a must that I dedicate this book to the very reflection and match of my own heart and soul, *mon chéri,* Alex.

There just aren't enough kisses and cashews to thank you properly for all of your love, belief, trust, inspiration, patience, encouragement, and dedication. You share your light with me so that I may share my colors with the world. For a gift as life changing as you I am forever grateful. *Merci beaucoup, chéri; je t'aime!*

To our firstborn baby, Nova, I look forward to feeding every ounce of your growing being, belly, heart, soul, and mind with love!

I have so much gratitude for my agent, Jeff Silberman. Thank you for discovering my potential and believing in this project. It's beyond touching to me to not just have any agent but one who operates from the heart and soul, all the while being an incredibly grounded businessperson. It has been a dream come true to work with you and have you and your family in my life!

This book wouldn't be half of what it is if it weren't for the amazingly talented Daryn Eller, who took my stories and recipes and wrote them in the most elegant of words. Daryn, you are an inspiration to me and have taught me so much about being a better writer. Your patience, flexibility, trust, and belief in this project were as valuable to me as your impressive writing skills. I am beyond grateful to have had the opportunity to work with you and connect with another creative Venetian.

You bring out the beauty in me, Christiane, both for the work you do with your trusty lens and for being a vibrant, loyal, honest, funny, and creative friend. I am very blessed to have worked with you on this project; it's a true gift to have created this book with a good friend. Thank you for all of your gorgeous photographs and for helping me eat copious amounts of dessert.

Olivia, you are my rock and the engine of PatisseRaw. I can't thank you enough for your years of dedication and service to my mission of providing healthful desserts to all who seek them. It is a great pleasure to work alongside you and share stories with you! You've truly become family to me! Thank you for recipe testing and jumping in wherever needed to make this book possible.

To my community here in Venice Beach, California: I am blessed to live near the ocean and sand and among the artists and abundant creativity that this community encapsulates. Thank you for feeding my spirit with so much gratitude and inspiration. I have never been touched so much by a place; you have my heart. Perhaps it is also because of you that I really got to know my heart.

To my loving mother and supportive father: you've both been inspiring me to create in the kitchen since before I was born, and no matter how much I resisted cooking for myself you somehow knew I'd grow into it. Thank you for always giving me the freedom to fly, live, learn, and grow. If it weren't for your dedication and inspiration I wouldn't be the woman I am today. Thank you, Mom, for being the first person to feed me with love, and to both of you for continuing to do so.

To my sisters—for your support with my sometimes crazy-sounding endeavors, thank you! I truly appreciate the feedback you offer and for sharing my treats with our growing family, especially all of my adorable nephews.

Merci beaucoup to my French family, especially Jennifer and Eric, for encouraging and supporting my projects with open and honest feedback, recipe testing, and belief in my talents. I am grateful that you share my work overseas and I am beyond blessed to have you in my life. Thank you for introducing me to Paris and all the patisseries, beauty, culture, and inspiration it has to offer.

To my dearest friends, who enrich not only my life but also every dessert that I create. Thank you for always trying my creations and supporting my endeavors. Your presence in my life is the sweetest treat of all. I love you all so very much!

Much gratitude to Jason Mraz for his delicious Chocomole recipe contribution.

To all my clients who have ever attended a class, bought my desserts, commented on my blog, shared my recipes, or supported PatisseRaw or Love-Fed, I thank you with every ounce of my heart. Without your support and presence in my life this dream would not be what it is today. I owe it all to you for guiding me on this journey, mentoring me, and supporting me. I believe we have co-created a movement that is far bigger than words can explain.

A very special thank-you to all the stores, cafes, and farmers' markets that I've had the pleasure of doing business with over the years, especially Gabe Dupin of Whole Foods Market.

Last, but certainly not least, thank you to everyone at BenBella Books, including Heather Butterfield, Adrienne Lang, Lindsay Marshall, and Sarah Dombrowsky, who have played a crucial role in making this project possible. Thank you for believing in this book and guiding and supporting it the whole way through. A special thank-you to Glenn Yeffeth for following his heart, creating this beautiful publishing house, and attracting a vibrant team of talented and passionate individuals. I am constantly in awe, pinching myself that I have the pleasure of collaborating with truly magnificent professionals.

INTRODUCTION

One of the best ways I know to give somebody joy is to dish up a serving of dessert. Desserts make people happy! They're offerings of love. Each time I dispatch a batch of cupcakes, assemble a pie, or churn a quart of ice cream, I feel like I'm preparing to send off little portions of bliss.

Now it's your turn to spread the love.

In this book, you'll find everything you need to create sweets that make people (including yourself) swoon. The fact that every *Love Fed* dessert—from the cakes and shakes to the puddings and parfaits—is made with nutritious ingredients that actually contribute to your well-being is just, well, the icing on the cake. Not that anyone will notice—biting into one of these treats is more likely to evoke thoughts of "heavenly" rather than "healthy." Still, it's nice to know that along with pure pleasure, with these desserts you're also serving up a big dollop of good-for-you-ness free of animal products (honey being the sometime exception), gluten, and unhealthy processed ingredients.

Although all the desserts in *Love Fed* are raw as well as beegan or vegan, they're not healthy substitutes for the "real thing." They *are* the real thing—indulgences that not only stand on their own but also delight people who happily eat traditional dairy- and egg-based sweets just as much as they thrill the people who happily don't. I think it may help, though, if I explain what I mean by raw, vegan, and beegan, just so you know what lies ahead. My definition of raw is food that has not been heated above 108°F. Because of the absence of heat, this food retains enzymes, hormones, vitamins, and minerals that might otherwise be lost. To me, raw food is simply more "alive." When I use the term "vegan," I'm referring to food that contains no animal products whatsoever: no eggs, no dairy, and of course, no meat. Beegans make an exception for honey. It's an animal product but can be produced in a very kind and sustainable way. Truthfully, I hate to put any kind of label on my own food, but if you must, call these *Love Fed* desserts equal-opportunity sweets—deliciousness for all!

Mostly, I just like to think of *Love Fed* desserts as modern. While inspired by both French pastries and conventional classics, they are thoroughly in step with the way more people are eating today. Many of us are not only interested in where our food comes from and how it affects our bodies, but we're also open to—and curious about—new ways of preparing what we eat. As much as desserts are comfort foods—and the *Love Fed* treats are no exception—it's exciting to get out of your cooking comfort zone and explore other ingredients and techniques. If this will be your first time making desserts without baking, I think you'll find that it's easy, fun, and very forgiving (preparing raw desserts doesn't demand the same nerve-wracking precision that baking does). Novices needn't feel intimidated, and seasoned cooks may even learn a new trick or two.

None of the *Love Fed* recipes requires any special equipment, and needless to say you don't even have to turn on your oven—no ingredient gets heated past 108°F in order to keep their nutritional profile as high as possible. These raw desserts also make use of an almost completely different portfolio of ingredients than conventional sweets do. If you've never used unrefined sweeteners like coconut sugar and agave, healthy fats like cacao and almond butters, dairy substitutes like coconut milk (yes, you can make ice cream with it!), and white flour swaps like almond flour, you're in for a treat. In this book, even the familiar—fruit, nuts, seeds, and dates—get used in new ways. For example, in a recipe contributed by Jason Mraz, one of my inspirations and favorite musicians, avocado is used as a base for pudding! Some ingredients may sound exotic, but they're actually all easily found at local stores or on the internet (just in case some items elude you, I'll clue you in on substitutions, too).

It used to be that delectable desserts were incompatible with the idea of eating for vitality, energy, and good health. Not anymore. *Love Fed* is here to ensure that you really *can* have your cake and eat it, too!

Desserts Made the *Love Fed* Way

The name *Love Fed* refers to both the love I put into my food and the love the earth gives to us by producing so many wonderful ingredients (I write a blog with the same name). It also relates to my philosophy about eating. Right now there's a tendency to fall into food camps: raw, vegan,

beegan, vegetarian, pescatarian . . . the list goes on. My feeling is that many of us are trying to do the best we can to eat conscientiously and that judging one another on our food choices separates, rather than unites, us. *Love Fed* desserts are all raw, but they are about options, too. For instance, some of the recipes use honey, but if you're vegan, you might want to replace it with another sweetener. Other ingredients, too, can be swapped out depending on your own particular preferences. These recipes are here to guide you, not mandate what you should be eating.

Consider this book, too, a primer on lesser-known ingredients and how to use them. I also want to share tips on how you can learn to prepare food in a more creative and intuitive way. If you're most comfortable sticking to a recipe, don't worry; every recipe in the book has step-by-step details. But if you're bold and like the idea of coming up with your own variations, I'll give you ideas on how to let your creative juices flow. Having the confidence to deviate from a recipe can help with practicalities—know how to make substitutions and you'll never have to worry about running out of, say, coconut milk, again—as well as free you to create your own masterpieces. If your kitchen strikes you as a dull or intimidating place—maybe just a means to an edible end—then I urge you to open your heart and mind to this luscious, raw, plant-based adventure.

Any way you slice it, *Love Fed* desserts are made with integrity, passion, and awareness. They're designed to nourish the body and satisfy the sweet tooth, and most of all to spread joy.

The Accidental Baker

In 2008, I traded in my business suits for a food processor and a life of culinary adventures. I mean I *literally* traded three elegantly tailored suits for a Hamilton Beach processor probably worth about $30. I like to think I got the better end of the deal.

At the time, I was working as a corporate recruiter, a job I fell into after a disappointing stint at a fashion school. Since the school substituted showing reruns of *Project Runway* for actual teaching, I felt I had no choice but to quit. Nervous as I was to leave school, that jump was nothing compared to the leap of faith I took when I left my solid, well-paying job to explore brave new gastronomic worlds. And yet it couldn't have worked out better: it wasn't long before I was selling my line of raw and vegan desserts to Whole Foods and local cafes around town. That was something no one who knew me—including myself—would have ever expected.

I consider myself somewhat of an accidental baker, as someone who went from doing no cooking at all to running a food business. It was like getting in a car and going from zero to sixty in the blink of an eye. Fast! I do, though, have a little bit of cooking DNA in my genes. When I was born, both my mother and my father were working as bakers. They'd met while training to be hairstylists several years after my mother had moved to the United States from Italy. But after they married, they both took jobs as bakers.

One of the great joys of my youth was watching my father as he made calzones, pizzas, cookies, and cakes, splashing flour everywhere as he cooked, yet also handling the dough super gently (especially for such a big guy). I loved helping my parents in the kitchen, but I never had a knack for the technical tasks involved. Timing, meticulous measurements, and all the other precise requirements of baking never resonated with me. So, instead, I simply stuck to decorating, filling, embellishing, and devouring their baked creations. Especially that last one—I was a very grateful recipient of my parents' baking expertise.

It wasn't just baking that I shied away from. Until I began playing around with dessert recipes, I never cooked anything for anyone. I didn't even cook for myself, relying instead on friends, family, and roommates to feed me, doing the dishes in return. When I first met Alex, my partner in both life and business, I could barely make toast without burning it!

The series of events that eventually led me to write *Love Fed* began with a period of detoxing. Early in our relationship, Alex and I decided to embark on a journey into what you might call alternative eating. We'd thought about doing the Master Cleanse— an all-liquid diet—but, frankly, we didn't think two active people such as ourselves could hack it. Instead, we decided to try a raw food cleanse. Just for two weeks. That was the deal.

We began by eating only foods prepared at 108°F or below and also crossed dairy, gluten, grains, meat, seafood, and sugar off our list of acceptable foods. What we were mostly left with was salads, guacamole, salsas, and smoothies. At least in the beginning. Once we got the hang of preparing meals in a raw way we started making things like vegetable lasagna and zucchini spaghetti and things got decidedly more interesting. For breakfast we would make what we called squirrel plates that consisted of banana, nut butters, hemp or flaxseeds, and raw chocolate and nuts. This unconventional but completely delicious meal would fuel us up until lunchtime when we'd usually have a salad. Midday we'd often have a snack of guacamole or hummus scooped up with endive leaves. For dinner, we'd get a bit fancier, creating pesto or salsa to toss with raw veggies like portobello mushrooms or zucchini.

The two weeks we'd committed to flew by, and then, before we knew it, two weeks turned into two months, then four, and we just kept on going. Both of us were amazed at how energetic and clear-headed we felt; we were waking up at five in the morning, full of ideas and eager to get on with our day. We shed pounds and gained insight. It was a revelation.

There was only one problem. After a while, our cravings for something sweet and indulgent became hard to ignore. Fruit just wasn't cutting it; we needed *real* dessert. In the old days, before committing myself to eating a raw, plant-based diet, I might have just walked to the corner store and grabbed an ice-cream bar. That wasn't an option anymore, so one day, more as an act of desperation than anything else, I took out an old blender and began contemplating what I could possibly make that would allow me to stay committed to my new way of life, yet also satisfy the overwhelming urge for sweetness I couldn't seem to shake. I opened the cupboard. Following my intuition (and the limitations of what was there), I threw some cacao powder, vanilla, bananas, coconut oil, cashews, and a little agave syrup into the blender and gave it a whirl. Then, with some trepidation, I took a taste.

Yum! It tasted so delightful that I shocked myself. Was it deprivation talking? Maybe it just tasted so good because I had abstained from sweets for so long. Alex had gone out surfing and I couldn't wait for him to come back and give me his opinion. In the meantime, I put the concoction into the refrigerator and it developed a pudding-like consistency that made it even better. Alex not only liked it, but he also encouraged me to keep experimenting.

In the months that followed I spent hours trying out new recipes, failing and succeeding in equal measure, and trying to learn from my mistakes as I went along. Still at my corporate recruiting job at the time, I'd bring my creations into the office and share them with my colleagues, asking for their feedback in return. Taking my inspiration from conventional classics, I began making raw, plant-based versions of cinnamon rolls, cheesecakes, and ice cream, only to find that they were far superior in taste, texture, and, of course, nutrition than the desserts that had inspired them. One of my earliest creations was tiramisu, a nod to my Italian heritage, and it, too, seemed refreshingly superior and delicious. Suddenly, I was eating sweets more than ever before; at times, I even ate them for breakfast (it was research!).

Because Alex is from France and grew up in Paris, he had exacting standards for pastries, which allowed him to serve as a wonderful critic and food tester extraordinaire. And because he loves me and wanted me to succeed (and because he's French!), he was always honest. Eventually, I got to a point where what I was doing felt like more than just fun—it was a calling. Now I just had to get up the courage to turn it into something other than a delicious hobby.

My first step was to test it out on the greater public. On busy art walk and event days, Alex and I would stand out on Abbot Kinney Boulevard, the main drag in our Venice Beach neighborhood, and hand out samples of desserts. People liked them—loved them even—but would they pay for them? The positive response convinced me that they would. I just had to figure out how to turn it into a business.

I quickly learned that creating a start-up food company (even a teeny, tiny one) is no simple task. Once I made the decision to embark on this wild ride, I asked everyone I knew (and many people I didn't) for advice. Nirvana was discovering that my neighbor was director of the Health Department, Wholesale Division—that is, he was the guy with all the insider information on running a food business. Nirvana, though, quickly turned to dejection once my neighbor graciously came over one evening and gave me the lowdown on what it would take to get up and running. The fees! The health rules! The horror stories about people who don't follow the guidelines! By the time he left, I was in tears.

And yet, I persevered. Then, remarkably, things started coming together. I needed to create a home test kitchen, a prohibitively expensive project, but one day, while walking down the street, Alex found stainless steel countertops that someone had put out with the trash. On another day I stumbled upon stainless steel storage racks and a rolling rack also abandoned on the street. It was as if fate was willing me into a life of making delectable desserts. One thing that I believe deeply, and which guides me to this day, is that you have everything you need at a given moment. It was like that first day of dessert making when I opened up my cupboard and found all the ingredients I needed to create something delicious—and change the course of my life. Now here I was, quitting my job, trading my suits for a food processor, and signing the lease on space in a commercial kitchen. Before I knew it, Alex and I had maxed out our credit cards and christened our new dessert business PatisseRaw, a play on the French word *patisserie*. What magic!

Still, I had to get back to reality. How were we going to get these great-tasting, good-for-you treats into stores? Together we began approaching small natural foods markets to see if they'd carry PatisseRaw, until Alex encouraged me to put aside my jitters and talk to store managers on my own. "You've got it; you can do it alone," he said, and so I did. I'll never forget the day I approached the Holy Grail—Whole Foods—with just my samples and ambition along for company. "Do they sell?" asked the buying manager. "Yes," I said, even though I'd never sold them in a store before! Fortunately, my little fib (or wishful thinking, as I prefer to call it) panned out. Once Whole Foods started stocking my chocolate, mango, and raspberry cake bites, as well as my carrot cupcakes, they flew off the shelves. Now we really *were* in business.

Even as making desserts has become my livelihood, one thing hasn't changed: I still use the same creative process to develop new desserts as I did back when it was just fooling around in my home kitchen. I set an intention to create something loving and pure that will bring happiness to others, but if ideas aren't flowing, I walk out of the kitchen. Coming up with new ideas for food is the same as any artistic endeavor, in that putting pressure on yourself to create something when all the signs are telling you it's not the right time only results in work you're ultimately not happy with. But when the timing is right? You can count on something delicious!

That's a bit of wisdom I hope you'll take with you whenever you decide to take one of the *Love Fed* recipes and turn it into a dessert that's uniquely your own—which I heartily encourage you to do. Maybe you'll even be inspired to write your own recipes from scratch. I hope you will. I can say from experience that it's a doubly satisfying experience. How many endeavors enable you to feel the thrill of creation *and* get something scrumptious to eat in the bargain?

The *Love Fed* Pantry

When feeding yourself and others, it's vital to use ingredients with integrity. Choosing as many organic, pesticide-free, and locally sourced ingredients as possible will help ensure that you are putting the very best nature has to offer on the table. Ground zero for these healthy ingredients is farmers' markets, where you can always find local and seasonal ingredients. Farmers' markets are also breeding grounds for creativity. With all the vibrant produce at its peak time, it's hard not to get excited thinking about what you can create with these finds.

As much as I like to buy local ingredients, I do make some exceptions, especially because many of the foods that make plant-based eating so wonderful come from places (like the tropics) where few of us are lucky enough to live. When buying ingredients from other countries, it's best to source them from a company that has visited the farms or done extensive research into the growing, processing, and handling of the food. For instance, I love using Essential Living Foods (which offers products like nuts, seeds, and cacao) because I know that Kipp, the owner, visits farms and reports back with videos and newsletters informing customers of what he's discovered. It's not always possible to get so much information, but it's quite comforting when you can.

If you're new to raw and plant-based cooking, you'll likely be unfamiliar with many of the ingredients. Just think of them as the new staples. Whereas flour, sugar, butter, baking powder, and baking soda are the basics used to make most conventional desserts, ingredients like cacao butter, coconut oil, coconut cream, agave nectar, and Irish moss are the foundation upon which no-bake, vegan sweets are built. I think that once you get used to them, they'll seem as ubiquitous as salt and pepper.

There are also many ingredients called for in the book that will need no introduction; you've probably used them many times before. I won't list them here, but I've created a little primer to help familiarize you with those newer staples. I think you'll have as much fun trying them out as a kid with a new chemistry set. And rest assured that they're all very easy to use and can be found in most natural—and even some traditional—food stores, or ordered online (unless otherwise noted). On page 227, you'll find a resource list that will help make sourcing the ingredients even easier.

On a final note, many of the recipes in *Love Fed* use nuts. Whenever nuts are called for, use the raw kind rather than roasted.

AGAVE NECTAR This sweetener comes from the beautiful agave succulents (which are the source of tequila, too). It's very sweet, so you need to use only a little bit of it, and it's not as thick as honey, so it makes a nice addition to ice tea. Some people worry about the fact that agave contains a lot of fructose, just like high-fructose corn syrup. But because I only use agave in small amounts, I'm not concerned that it will drive up blood sugar the way that other high-fructose sweeteners do. Use it sparingly and agave nectar is a perfectly safe sweetener.

Substitution option: Feel free to use your favorite liquid sweetener (such as maple syrup) wherever agave is called for, as most syrup sweeteners substitute one-to-one.

CACAO BUTTER Pressed from the cacao bean—dried, partly fermented fatty seeds of a South American evergreen tree—cacao butter (also known as cocoa butter) is a healthy vegetable fat with a chocolaty aroma. The butter is the fatty part of cacao pressed out of and separated from the bean. It's most commonly used as the base for chocolate confections, but cacao butter can also be used directly on the skin as a moisturizer. Since it has a long shelf life (three to five years) it's often included in beauty products. Pregnant women can use cacao butter to help prevent stretch marks. Besides natural food stores and online suppliers, shops that sell candy-making supplies often sell cacao butter.

CACAO NIBS These little bits of raw chocolate are chipped right from the bean, lightly roasted, and hulled. They're used in ways similar to chocolate chips, though they have no sweetener added, and are often used to produce different grades of commercial chocolate. The nibs are slightly bitter and may be sweetened with honey or used in baked goods; they make a great snack, too. Some research suggests that cacao nibs and the dark grades of chocolate made from them benefit the digestive system, heart and blood vessels, and blood sugar levels.

Substitution option: Use pure unsweetened dark chocolate chips.

CACAO POWDER This isn't a misspelling: I meant to write cacao rather than cocoa powder. While they are similar, cacao powder is typically minimally processed, so it maintains higher levels of antioxidants and minerals than cocoa powder does. It also contains no sugar or milk and hasn't been heated to extreme temperatures. Like cocoa powder, though, cacao powder can be used in all manner of dessert making. Along with the usual places noted in the introduction to this section, cacao powder can sometimes be found in shops selling candy-making supplies.

Substitution option: Cocoa powder is an easier to find, and often cheaper, option. For every tablespoon of cacao powder, substitute 1 tbsp. of cocoa powder. (Look for a powder in its purest form without any sugar or additives.)

CHIA SEEDS These tiny seeds, packed with omega-3 fatty acids, protein, fiber, calcium, and iron, can be added to foods for crunch or hydrated to add thickness. When wet, chia seeds release a viscous gel that can replace milk and cream in puddings and add body to other desserts. Chia gel also makes an excellent egg replacement for vegan baking. The seeds, available in both black and white, are also known for providing stamina: Aztec warriors used them for energy, and they're still popular with long-distance runners.

COCONUT When you buy a whole coconut, you're getting a lot: both the water and the meat are a great addition to desserts. Coconut also has incredible health benefits. Besides being low in calories and high in heart-healthy fats, it helps soften skin, potentially slow aging, and even protect against the sun's damaging rays.

Fresh coconuts may look daunting if you're not used to them, but they're easy to crack and use. To select a good coconut, first feel its weight—despite their size, many large coconuts actually don't contain much water or meat. For the best value, strive to find the heaviest coconut regardless of size. I also check the bottom of a coconut to see whether it's soggy; if I can puncture it easily with my finger I put it back and look for one that's firmer. Firm coconuts lend extra creaminess and a smooth texture to recipes.

Asian markets tend to sell coconuts for half the price of regular markets. Buying coconuts in bulk is also a great way to save money. When I buy a dozen or more I immediately take them home and crack them open (I'll admit I was scared to do so my very first time but now I look forward to it). I then pour out the water and scoop out the meat with a spoon. I pour the water into ice cube trays and place the meat in a bag and store both in the freezer until ready to use. Both frozen coconut meat and coconut water are great in shakes and smoothies. And once you try fresh coconut, you'll never want to go back to canned.

Tips for opening a fresh coconut (see photos opposite): Place the coconut on its side on a flat, sturdy surface. Hold a large chef's knife in your dominant hand and steady the coconut with your other, being careful to keep your fingers out of the way of the knife. Shave the top of the coconut fiber down toward the top point of the coconut, working your way completely down to the shell. Once you see the darker brown shell under the fiber, place the coconut upright and using the heel of your knife, tap the shell until a crack appears. Once a crack forms chances are the whole top will lift off, but if you have a difficult coconut, continue cracking around the shell until you're able to lift the corner of the coconut top with your knife and remove the top so you can pour out the water. Once the coconut is empty of water, scoop out the flesh with a metal spoon. Peel away any hard shell remaining on the back of the flesh (I recommend using a paring knife to do this part if necessary) and give the flesh a rinse under cool water to help any shell debris move along.

COCONUT CREAM Coconut cream is commonly used to turn puddings and frostings velvety. You can simply skim the cream off the top of a can of whole-fat coconut milk (see page 227) or buy cans of pure coconut cream (no skimming required). Look for it in Asian markets (they have the best variety and lowest prices) or regular grocery stores, being sure to purchase only those brands with no sweeteners or additives.

COCONUT CRYSTALS Coconut crystals are commonly referred to as palm sugar. This sugar replacement is made from coconut nectar that is dried at a low temperature. It can be used as a one-to-one replacement for either white or brown sugar. I often grind it down to an even finer consistency using a food processor or coffee/spice grinder when I want to ensure a smooth finish to a dessert. Unlike most types of

sugar, coconut sugar has a high mineral content: it's rich in potassium, magnesium, zinc, and iron.

COCONUT NECTAR This sweetener comes from the sap of the coconut tree and is retrieved much like maple syrup: by tapping the tree. Coconut nectar is unprocessed, which leaves its considerable vitamins, minerals, and enzymes intact. It has a viscosity much like molasses—it's very thick and sticky—and can be used as a one-to-one replacement for any other liquid sweetener.

COCONUT OIL I use coconut oil to add viscosity and shape to a recipe, making a "cheese" cake firm up, for instance, as the coconut oil solidifies. It was long thought that coconut oil was unhealthy because it has a high saturated fat content. On further investigation, it was found that the type of saturated fat in coconut oil is metabolized much differently than the saturated fat in animal foods. So, far from unhealthy, coconut oil can actually enhance your well-being.

And it isn't just a great dessert ingredient. Coconut oil is also an excellent moisturizer for your skin and hair, and something most people don't know: it makes a wonderful mouthwash by "pulling" bacteria from the mouth. Using coconut oil as a mouthwash involves putting about a tablespoon of oil in your mouth, then swishing it around your teeth for 10 to 20 minutes. During this process, bacteria get " stuck" and dissolve in the liquid oil. Who would have thought?

DATES Dates, it must be said, are not especially beautiful, but do they ever taste delicious! While they're probably not unfamiliar to you, these palm tree jewels are frequently underused. Boy, did I have a lot to learn about dates when I first started using them in desserts. Once I got the hang of it, though, it became clear that dates are the ultimate binding agent for crusts, a delicious addition to smoothies and shakes, and a versatile snack when you're craving a simple sweet. Dates come in a variety of different types and flavors, ranging from a deep caramel taste to a rich honey. In some recipes, I recommend a particular date; in others, I leave it up to you. Dates can be found in most grocery stores, health food stores, and even in bulk sections, but my favorite place to buy dates is from the farmers' markets (a luxury of living in Southern California). Not only do you get to sample all the varieties, but also you often get them freshly picked. Dates have a long shelf life, so sometimes store-bought dates can be from last year's crop. That's not necessarily a bad thing, but the fresher your dates, the better.

HEMP SEEDS Hemp seeds can be eaten raw, ground into a meal, sprouted, made into hemp milk (akin to soy milk), prepared as tea, and used in baking. Hemp is rich in amino acids (it's close to a complete protein) and is nature's highest botanical source of essential fatty acids, over flax or any other nut or seed oil. I love using it just as one would use sprinkles on cupcakes, ice cream, smoothies, and just about anything that you like to decorate. Unlike sprinkles, it gives your desserts a nutritional boost and subtle nutty flavor.

HONEY Many vegans don't use honey; it is, after all, produced by living creatures. I, though, do use honey on occasion—nothing quite replaces its unique flavor and viscosity. I feel it is very important to buy raw unpasteurized honey and, even more importantly, to source it from local and small beekeepers who follow ethical practices. Raw honey is antifungal, antibacterial, antiviral, and rich in beneficial enzymes and vitamins. When and if you choose to consume honey, be aware that its pureness is often identifiable by its viscosity and shelf life. Raw honey will sink to the bottom of a glass of water and can even be lit on fire; processed honey is usually much too moist to catch fire and it dissolves in water. Also, raw honey will crystalize over time; processed honey will remain syrupy for long periods of time. Talk to your local beekeepers at farmers' markets and get familiar with their practices so you can make educated decisions on honey.

Aside from using honey in your desserts, it also makes a wonderful body scrub and face wash. Combine 2 tsp. ground almonds and 2 tsp. honey to form a paste. Gently rub onto your face in a circular motion. Rinse with warm water. For a whole body scrub, simply increase the amount of almonds and honey.

IRISH MOSS When people come over and I have Irish moss soaking on my countertop, they're always intrigued, wondering what it is and what I use it for. The look on their faces when I tell them it's in the cake they just ate is priceless. But you can't blame anyone for being a little averse to Irish moss on first sight. It comes full of sand and has an ocean-like smell that instantly teleports you to the beach. But once you rinse and soak it, Irish moss transforms into an amazing natural thickener. If you've ever had carrageenan (it's in tons of products, including ice cream and yogurt), you've had Irish moss; you just didn't know it.

You can add Irish moss to any recipe you want to make thicker, smoother, or creamier. It works very well in cake, ice cream, pudding, and shake recipes, taking the texture to a whole new level but without adding any unwanted flavor. As a plus, Irish moss also has a high mineral content. Soaked (see page 28), it will keep in the fridge for up to three days. To maintain its purity, always change the water daily (or things can get stinky fast).

LUCUMA What on planet earth is lucuma? That's what I asked when I was first introduced to this sweet ingredient. Lucuma is a soft, Peruvian fruit with a caramel-like flavor. It most commonly comes in powder form and is used quite often in Peru for ice cream and desserts. In fact, in Peru, lucuma ice cream is just as popular as chocolate and vanilla. I love using lucuma in smoothies, ice creams, shakes, cakes, sauces, and chocolates.

MACA POWDER Grown in the Andes, maca is a nourishing, energizing plant and a staple of Peruvian cuisine. It was prized by the Inca for its ability to balance the endocrine system and aid the body in coping with stress. My favorite use of maca powder is in shakes, smoothies, and juices. It can also be easily mixed into baked goods and pancake batter. I especially love the way it pairs with chocolate. Together the two really help balance out hormones—it may be the placebo effect, but it truly works!

MATCHA POWDER Matcha is finely milled green tea. It adds a delicate earthy flavor to foods and is particularly rich in a type of antioxidant called catechins, known to help prevent cancer. Tea shops often carry matcha powder, but you can also find it in Asian and natural food stores.

ORANGE BLOSSOM WATER This clear, perfumed distillation of fresh bitter-orange blossoms is a delicate way to add unique flavor to your favorite dessert recipe. I came across this ingredient on my first trip to Paris. I was shopping for nuts to make a raw dessert and I noticed rose water and orange blossom water on the shelves of a charming Israeli market. I knew I had to take them back to the States for culinary experimentation. Pleased by the results, I began to look for these products in the United States and found that they are common at most European and ethnic markets.

Note: Many natural food stores also carry orange blossom and rose waters, and I've recently discovered them in the liquor and beauty aisles of traditional markets as well.

ROSE WATER Rose water is a fragrant liquid that you can use to give desserts a flowery note (it makes a great facial toner, too). See the note under Orange Blossom Water to learn more about where to find it.

VANILLA BEAN POWDER Many of the recipes in this book give you the option of using vanilla bean powder instead of vanilla extract. It's my personal preference because it's undiluted, so you get a lot of vanilla flavor in every spoonful. Be sure to buy pure vanilla powder because some brands are combined with sweeteners or are synthetic extracts.

Kitchen Essentials

You don't need to have much—or top-of-the-line—equipment to create the desserts in this book. As you might remember, I started Love-Fed with the help of little more than a $30 food processor. I do recommend, however, that you begin by having at least a blender and some kind of food processor; even a mini will do.

Like me, you may find that as you progress with cooking it makes sense to upgrade your equipment. The food processor I traded my business suits for was small and rudimentary and, for a newbie, it was perfect. But when I really wanted to sharpen my dessert-making craft, I began looking into professional-grade machines and tools. This more expensive equipment seemed more fun to work with and offered better results, and it actually made economic sense. Lower-priced machines tend to need replacing every few years if you use them a lot, so laying out more money up front ultimately made sense. If you're craving more expensive equipment but find it's beyond your budget, consider reaching out to friends, family, and co-workers. (Craigslist.org is a good resource, too.) Many people splurge on top machines only to never use them. Perhaps you can borrow, trade (desserts are an excellent bartering tool), or find a bargain in order to get them into your kitchen.

The following list of equipment is basic with some suggestions for items that can take your dessert making to a higher level. To make it clear which tools you can do without, I've listed them as optional. Keep in mind how often you'll be making desserts and stock up accordingly.

BLENDER Any regular blender will enable you to make the recipes in this book, but as with the food processor, the better your blender, the more you'll get out of it (and the longer it will last). I've tried many different blenders, ranging from a very vintage Oster with buttons missing to a stick blender to a Magic Bullet. They all get the job done. But when it comes to getting a light whipped texture and a soft consistency, you can't beat a high-speed Vitamix. This machine, which runs into the hundreds of dollars but is extremely reliable and powerful, can also blend a quick ice cream or lightly warm a sauce. Depending on where you are in your culinary journey, buying a Vitamix may be something you want to consider.

CITRUS ZESTER (OPTIONAL) This convenient tool allows you to finely remove the skin from citrus fruit without getting any of the bitter pith. If you don't have one, a fine grater or paring knife will do.

DEHYDRATOR (OPTIONAL) A dehydrator is a machine that dries out food at a very low temperature. It can be used to gently warm food, too. I recommend starting out with a machine that has at least four to six trays. Dehydrating can take a lot of time, so it's most efficient to dry large batches at once. I prefer a machine that is quiet, has round shapes (for making fruit roll-ups and pizza crusts), is designed for even drying (meaning trays don't need to be rotated), and has a built-in timer.

ELECTRIC MIXER (OPTIONAL) Both stand and handheld electric mixers are wonderful for creating a light, airy base for cakes and cookies. If you don't have either, a food processor or whisk (and a strong, tireless hand) can fill in.

FOOD PROCESSOR I started out with a simple Hamilton Beach food processor and, at the time, it got the job done well. However, I learned that smaller machines are not well suited to the constant blending of nuts and that I was shortening the life span of the tool by doing so. Sure enough, after a lot of experimenting I blew the motor. I later went on to own a Cuisinart food processor, which has a lot of advantages, including a larger bowl, stronger motor, and sharper blade suited for chopping nuts. The price for food processors can vary greatly depending on quality. If you plan to use one every day I recommend investing in a Cuisinart, especially when you buy it from a store (such as Sur La Table) that offers a good warranty and (if you're thinking about going pro) a discount for people in the food business.

GRATER Many recipes call for grated ginger or shaved chocolate. This will do the trick.

ICE-CREAM MAKER (OPTIONAL) It's possible to make frozen treats without an ice-cream maker and, as you'll see, all the recipes in this book give an alternative method. However, you'll achieve the best results with an ice-cream maker, which allows you to avoid excessive ice crystals and create the smoothest texture. I have a Cuisinart ice-cream maker, which creates an evenly churned ice cream in less than 30 minutes. Cuisinart makes a range of models, beginning at fairly low prices.

ICE-CREAM SCOOP (OPTIONAL) Sure, a spoon will do, but if you want to get that ice-cream parlor look we all know and love, it's nice to have an ice-cream scoop. I prefer a nice spring in my scoop—that extra push off from the scoop works well to ensure the perfect ball of goodness lands in the bowl or tops off a cupcake.

KNIVES It goes without saying that every kitchen needs knives, but I just want to note that having both small paring knives and chopping knives will serve you well.

MEASURING CUPS AND SPOONS From ultra-large cups for soaking ingredients to tiny spoons for measuring spices, a good set of measuring utensils is key. It's also helpful to have both liquid and dry measures. Having a glass Pyrex measuring cup with a spout comes in especially handy when making chocolates and sauces.

MIXING BOWLS You'll need mixing bowls of varying sizes for these recipes, mainly small, medium, and large, though having an extra-large one can be handy, too. I prefer metal bowls when working with all ingredients except for melted chocolate, which hardens quickly when it touches the cool metal (plastic works best for warm chocolate). Metal bowls can also fill in for a double boiler for melting cacao butter and coconut oil.

MUFFIN/CUCPAKE LINERS AND MOLDS These come in handy when making chocolates, mini cupcakes, and more. You'll need paper liners in a variety of sizes and colors for molding and embellishing the presentation of a dessert—the more festive, the better. I also often use reusable silicone molds. These are great when you just need to shape a treat and don't need a decorative finish.

NUT MILK BAG OR FINE-MESH STRAINER Some recipes require straining a mixture or an ingredient, and these are your best options. Nut milk bags in particular come in very handy when making nut milks (hence the name), but you can use these reusable fine-mesh bags for straining other things as well. I like them because they retain all the pulp in the bag, cutting down on mess and allowing you to easily preserve the pulp for other uses. A fine-mesh strainer can also work, though it's not as efficient as a nut milk bag. If you find yourself without either, use cheesecloth, tripled to create a fine mesh.

OFFSET SPATULA (OPTIONAL) What a versatile and underestimated tool! I can't imagine not having an offset spatula, which has a bent, thin metal blade used for smoothing surfaces, gently lifting cupcakes and doughnuts out of pans, and swirling frosting on cakes, among other jobs. Although it's possible to get by without one by using the back of a spoon or a butter knife, an offset spatula doesn't cost much and I highly recommend owning one. They come in a range of sizes; I have one that's 4½"—small, but just right. Be careful not to get one that's too flimsy, as it will make for sloppy lifting and spreading.

PANS AND MOLDS I adore a 9x9" square pan for making cakes, mostly because I love cutting the cakes into petite bites. I recommend, though, having a small selection of different shapes ranging from round to rectangular and even heart shaped. It will also be helpful to have a doughnut pan, cupcake pan, and loaf pan; however, they're not absolutely necessary: all of these shapes can also be formed by hand, and cupcakes can be made in liners. While each recipe in this book specifies the best pan size and shape to use, feel free to substitute other pans if you like. One of the many great things about making desserts without baking is that you don't have to worry about how pan size will affect cooking time.

PARCHMENT PAPER Many recipes in this book call for lining pans and bowls with parchment paper, which prevents sticking and, in some cases, will help you lift out a molded dessert. I also use parchment paper to wrap finished cookies and chocolates, as well as to line countertops for rolling out dough and working with sticky ingredients. Consider, too, that you can get four to six reuses out of one sheet of parchment, so a roll can last you a very long time.

PIE PLATE I have one pie dish that satisfies my every need. It's the perfect size (9") and made entirely of Pyrex glass. Glass chills nicely and looks beautiful enough to go from kitchen to table.

PIE SPATULA (OPTIONAL) I find a pie spatula helpful for transferring slices to the plate and for scooping out streusel and cobblers.

PIPING KIT (OPTIONAL) Visually speaking, the frosting bag and pastry tips in a piping kit can take your desserts to another level. If you don't want to spring for the whole kit, you can simply purchase frosting tips and use a plastic ziplock bag instead of a pastry bag.

ROLLING PIN (OPTIONAL) A simple acrylic, wood, or marble rolling pin will work well. Substitute a glass jar or can if you don't have one.

RUBBER SPATULAS AND SPOONS It's so much easier to get every last drop from your mixing bowls when you have a rubber- or silicone-tipped tool on hand. I recommend stocking your kitchen with two standard-size spatulas, one mini spatula, and one standard-size rubber spoon.

THE
RECIPES

ONE
LOVE FED BASICS

These simple techniques will help you navigate the *Love Fed* recipes and further your own exploration into cooking.

Basic Techniques

HOW TO MELT CACAO BUTTER

Using a grater, shave cacao butter into the top of a double boiler or a heatproof bowl. Place the double boiler or bowl over a pan of gently boiling water, stirring the cacao butter until melted.

> ♥ SAVOR THIS ♥
>
> Costa Rica is rife with cacao (chocolate) trees, and eating cacao fresh from the tree during a vacation there was one of the highlights of my trip. Alex and I spotted one down the road from the tree-house community where we were staying. Alex pulled over so I could talk to the farmers who had approximately twenty trees in their yard. One of them pulled two large bright yellow pods off the tree. He then proceeded to slice one open with his machete and hand it to me. We all admired its beauty and scent before taking a bite. The outer pod was hard and thick, a sturdy shell to protect the gelatinous beans inside. The fruit was white with a wet flesh feel that was slippery to the touch and silky feeling on the tongue. When I bit into it, I was shocked at how bitter and acidic it tasted. Sucking on the bean was like sucking on SweeTarts (without the sweet part)! I forgot that the bean has to ferment before it develops its chocolate flavor.

HOW TO MELT COCONUT OIL

It's possible to melt coconut oil without turning on a stove burner, by leaving it either in a sunny spot on your kitchen counter or on top of your stove. However, if neither of those techniques works in your kitchen, melt the coconut oil in a pot on the stove using very low heat and giving it an occasional stir, or by putting it in a bowl in the microwave for a few seconds. Placing it in a dehydrator works, too.

HOW TO MAKE COCONUT CREAM

Place a can of full-fat coconut milk in the refrigerator (or several cans—that way you'll have extra on hand when you need it). Chill for 24 hours. Open the can and scoop out the thick cream from the top, making sure to leave the water behind. Save the leftover coconut water for another use. One can usually yields about 1 c. coconut cream.

HOW TO SOAK IRISH MOSS

Place Irish moss in a jar and cover with water by 4". Allow to soak until it expands and takes on a lighter, almost translucent shade, which can take anywhere from 30 minutes to 4 hours. The moss is ready when it turns creamy white in color and nearly doubles in size and weight. Rinse and drain before using.

HOW TO SOAK NUTS

Rinse the nuts well under cold water. Place in a medium bowl and add cold water to cover by 2–3". Cover the bowl and place in a cool spot for 2–4 hours (if you have the time, go for the longer soak). Drain before using. Use nuts while damp. If you don't want to use all the nuts at one time, the remaining nuts can be dried in a dehydrator and stored for later use.

Basic Recipes

BASIC CASHEW CREAM

Yield: 3 c.
Prep time: 10 minutes, plus 2–4 hours soaking time

2 c. whole cashews, soaked and drained (above)

Rinse the cashews under cold water. Place in a blender with enough fresh cold water to cover by 1". Blend on high for several minutes until very smooth. If you're not using a professional high-speed blender such as a Vitamix, which creates an ultra-smooth cream, strain the cashew cream through a fine-mesh sieve or nut milk bag.

Use immediately or store in the refrigerator for up to 3 days or in the freezer for up to a month.

BASIC CASHEW ALMOND CREAM

Yield: Approximately 3 cups
Prep time: 5 minutes, plus 2–4 hours soaking time

1 c. almonds, soaked and drained (above)
1 c. cashews, soaked and drained (above)
²/₃ to 1 c. filtered water

Rinse the almonds and cashews under cold water. Place in a food processor or Vitamix or other high-speed blender with ²/₃ c. water. Blend until *very* smooth, adding more water if the mixture is not reaching a creamy consistency. You'll most likely need to blend for a full minute or longer.

If you are not using a high-speed blender, strain the cream through a nut milk bag or fine-mesh sieve. For a sweetened cream, blend the cream with dates, vanilla extract, vanilla bean, or maple syrup to taste.

Use immediately or store in the refrigerator for up to 3 days or in the freezer for up to a month.

BASIC NUT BUTTER

Yield: Approximately 1 cup
Prep time: 15 minutes

You can easily make your own nut butters from a variety of raw nuts—and for a fraction of the cost of store-bought. While they pair naturally with chocolate and desserts, try a dollop of do-it-yourself nut butters on ice cream or as a spread on cookies.

2 c. your favorite nut (such as almonds, jungle peanuts, hazelnuts, or cashews)

Place the nuts in a food processor and process until a butter forms. As you process the nut butter, bear in mind that it may take as long as 15 minutes. First you'll see coarse chunks of the nuts; soon after it will take on a flourlike consistency. Once it's become like a fine flour, scrape down the sides on occasion. Stop processing when the nut butter is smooth and creamy.

Use immediately or store in the refrigerator for up to 3 days or the freezer for up to a month.

Cashews being ground into cashew butter.

♥ TIPS & TRICKS ♥

Once you've tried the basic nut butter recipe, your own creativity becomes a main ingredi-ent. Try combining different nuts and adding natural flavorings to produce a range of deli-cious spreads. To try:

• Experiment with various combinations of nuts, including almonds, cashews, pecans, walnuts, pistachios, macadamia, or Brazil nuts.

• Add seeds, such as pumpkin or sunflower, and dried fruit like raisins.

• Add sweetness with honey, maple syrup, vanilla, cacao, cinnamon, or cardamom. Start small, adding, say, 1 tsp. honey or ¼ tsp. cinnamon.

• To create a creamier consistency, add 1 tsp. coconut oil (which will also give it a subtle tropical flavor) or flaxseed oil (for an omega-3 boost).

BASIC SWEETENED NUT MILK

Yield: 4 cups
Prep time: 10 minutes, plus 2–4 hours soaking time

Have fun and play around with using different nuts and seeds to make this milk. You can also try other sweeteners and flavorings, including cacao powder, cacao nibs, berries, and spices. It's surprisingly simple to make your own unique and flavorful milks.

1 c. soaked nuts (see page 29)
6 pitted dates or 2 tbsp. liquid sweetener
1 tsp. vanilla bean powder or vanilla extract
⅛ tsp. sea salt
4 c. filtered water

Place the nuts, dates, vanilla bean powder, sea salt, and water in a blender and blend until smooth. Strain through a fine-mesh sieve or nut milk bag into a glass jar. Set the pulp aside, and store the milk in the refrigerator for up to 3 days.

························ ♥ TIPS & TRICKS ♥ ·······························

What to Do with Leftover Nut Pulp:

- Dry out pulp and use it as flour in your dessert recipes. You can use an oven or a dehydrator to do so. If using the oven, set it on the lowest setting and allow the pulp to dry completely. If you have a dehydrator, spread the pulp on a cookie sheet and dry it at 108°F until dry. Drying times will vary depending on your oven or machine, but check it after 5 hours, then again every hour after that.

- Pulp also makes great compost for the garden.

- Freeze the pulp and use it to make crackers, cookies, or muffins.

BASIC CHOCOLATE BAR

Yield: 1 bar
Prep time: 30 minutes

This recipe will make a chocolate bar that you can grate or shave to garnish desserts. The chocolate can also be poured into molds (while still liquid) to create fun candies and molded garnishes for your desserts.

Note: If you'd prefer not to make your own chocolate, a cheaper and easier to find solution would be to use a pure dark chocolate bar that does not have added sugars or additives.

1 c. melted cacao butter (see page 27)
1 c. cacao powder
⅓ c. agave nectar
1 tsp. vanilla extract

Line a loaf pan or glass bowl with parchment paper or plastic wrap, allowing the paper or wrap to hang over the sides.

Place the melted cacao in a medium bowl and stir in the cacao powder, agave nectar, and vanilla extract. Mix until smooth. Pour the mixture into the lined pan and place in the freezer until firm, about 15 minutes.

Use immediately or store in the refrigerator for up to 3 days or in the freezer for up to a month.

BASIC CHOCOLATE SAUCE

Yield: 2 cups
Prep time: 5 minutes

1 c. cacao powder
1 c. coconut nectar
1 tbsp. melted coconut oil (see page 28)
1 tsp. vanilla extract

Combine the cacao powder, coconut nectar, coconut oil, and vanilla extract in a small bowl and mix well with a fork. Transfer to a squirt bottle for easy decorating, or use a fork to drizzle over desserts.

Use immediately or store in the refrigerator for up to 3 days. The mixture will harden with refrigeration, so when ready to use, set the squirt bottle or bowl of chocolate in a bowl of warm water or run under hot water to soften.

BASIC WHITE CHOCOLATE SAUCE

Yield: 2 cups
Prep time: 15 minutes, plus 2–4 hours soaking time

This chocolate can be used as a dip for berries, poured into chocolate molds to make candy, or used over cakes.

1 c. cashews, soaked and drained (see page 29)
1 tsp. vanilla extract
6 tbsp. agave nectar
2 tbsp. almond milk
1 c. melted cacao butter (see page 27)
1 tbsp. melted coconut oil (see page 28)

Place the cashews, vanilla extract, agave nectar, and almond milk in a blender and blend until smooth. Add the melted cacao butter and coconut oil. Blend lightly until well mixed and allow to sit for 5 minutes to thicken.

Use right away or store in the refrigerator for up to 3 days. The mixture will harden with refrigeration, so when ready to use, set the squirt bottle or bowl of chocolate in a bowl of warm water or run under hot water to soften.

BASIC CARAMEL SAUCE

Yield: Approximately 1 cup
Prep time: 10 minutes

Traditionally, caramel sauce is made with lots of cream, sugar, and butter—your arteries may harden just thinking about it! This sauce, on the other hand, is similarly rich and deep with flavor, but unlike regular caramel sauce it's good for your heart. It makes a nice complement to a morning hot cocoa, is lovely drizzled over ice cream, and can be used to create a delightfully gooey layer between brownies. It's also delicious as a dip for fruit.

1½ tbsp. melted cacao butter (see page 27)
¼ c. lucuma powder
¾ c. coconut nectar
1 tsp. butterscotch extract

Place the cacao butter in a small bowl and add the lucuma powder, coconut nectar, and butterscotch extract. Whisk with a fork until all clumps are gone and the mixture turns a caramel color. If necessary, to keep the sauce fluid, transfer (or leave) in a heatproof bowl and place over a pot of simmering water. If using a double boiler, simply return it to the pot. Use immediately.

BASIC DATE SYRUP

Yield: Approximately 1 cup
Prep time: 5 minutes, plus 30 minutes or more soaking time

This is a great sweetener to add to your collection. It can be used in place of agave nectar, coconut nectar, or honey in recipes and, by itself, makes an excellent substitute for jams and jellies.

15 pitted dates, soaked for at least 30 minutes or as long as overnight
1 c. filtered water
½ tsp. vanilla extract

Place the dates, water, and vanilla extract in a blender and blend until smooth. Transfer to an airtight jar. Store in the refrigerator for up to 3 weeks.

BASIC MACERATED FRUIT TOPPING

Yield: Variable, depending on your needs
Prep time: 5 minutes, plus 30 minutes or more soaking time

To take my fruity recipes to the next level of scrumptiousness, I often macerate the fruit, which simply means plumping it up or drawing out the moisture from the fruit using a syrup. Citrus is often added to brighten the flavor. This is a great way to prepare fruit that is not in peak season. Macerating also lends a glazed look to fruit, making it the perfect topping for cakes, ice creams, parfaits, puddings, and more. Served all by itself, it makes a quick and delicious snack.

You can use any fruit you like and any combination of syrups, herbs, and spices to macerate. Here are some elements to choose among:

Syrups: coconut nectar, honey, maple syrup, agave nectar
Ground or whole spices: cinnamon, black pepper, star anise, ginger
Citrus juice and zest
Fresh chopped herbs
Fresh or dried chiles
Extracts such as vanilla or almond

For every cup of fruit, add 2 tbsp. syrup and 1 tsp. citrus juice. Additionally, include herbs of your choosing, leaving them whole on the stem if you want to easily pick them out and discard. Or chop them fine and leave them in the mix. When using ginger it is best to peel and mince the ginger first. Soak fruit anywhere from 30 minutes to overnight in the refrigerator depending on how much time you have. (The soaked fruit becomes more flavorful as it absorbs the lemon and sweetener.) Serve immediately or store in the refrigerator for up to 3 days.

BASIC CRUST FOR CHEESECAKES AND PIES

Yield: One 9″ round crust
Prep time: 10 minutes

Creating a perfectly firm, crunchy-chewy crust requires only a few basic ingredients, and you can vary those ingredients according to your own tastes. First, you choose a base ingredient, usually a nut or seed. You can use a single type of nut or seed as a base or any combination of your favorites—either way, it's hard to go wrong. If you like a dense crust, I recommend using nutrient-rich buckwheat groats in place of nuts (soak them for 2–3 hours for optimal nutritional benefits and digestion). For a lighter crust, try using cashews. Almonds make a crunchy crust. My all-time favorite is a combination of almonds, pecans, and Brazil nuts.

Once you have the nuts/seeds selected, choose a binder. Dried fruits such as dates, raisins, apricots, or cranberries make excellent binders, as do liquid sweeteners like coconut nectar, maple syrup, agave, or yacon syrup. The goal is to find the right ratio of binder to base—that's what holds the crust together—so, depending on the moistness of your binder, you may have to play with the pro-portions to get the right balance. In the event your crust is not binding, add a little more dried fruit or sweetener, but just enough to help the ingredients stick together—too much and you'll end up with a mushy crust.

You can further customize your crust with flavor add-ins. Citrus zest, extracts like vanilla and almond, cacao powder, cacao nibs, and spices like cinnamon, ginger, and nutmeg all make wonderful addi-tions. You may also want to add a pinch of salt to help bring out the flavors. As with anything you create, let your imagination come out to play; just tweak the recipe as your taste buds dictate.

When pressing the crust into a pan, I find it easiest to keep my hands and especially my fingers moistened lightly with water to help prevent sticking. You can press the crust into the pan starting at the center and working outward, or vice versa; whichever way you go, the main objective is to press the crust as evenly as possible to create a clean finish and a level dessert.

1½ c. mixed nuts or seeds (e.g., ½ c. almonds, ½ c. Brazil nuts, ½ c. pecans)
¼ c. liquid sweetener or ½ c. dried fruit
1 tsp. vanilla bean powder or vanilla extract

Place the mixed nuts, liquid sweetener, and vanilla bean powder in a food processor and process until a fine crumble forms and sticks together. Remove the crust mixture from the processor and press into a pie or springform pan.

BASIC NATURAL FOOD COLORINGS

If your aim is to add some color to a frosting or cheesecake, use this food coloring guide to help create a bright finish. Keep in mind that a little of each ingredient (especially turmeric, saffron, beet juice, and matcha) goes a long way, so start with just a touch and go from there. Note that the fruits and vegetables mentioned should be pureed and strained or juiced to extract the color.

Green: Matcha powder, spinach, avocado
Red/pink: Raspberries, strawberries
Orange: Carrots
Fuchsia: Beets
Yellow: Golden beets, turmeric, saffron
Brown: Cacao powder
Purple/blue: Blueberries, blackberries

To create color using powders: Start by adding ¼ tsp. to frosting or batter, adding more as you go to adjust the color to your liking (but don't go overboard—powders such as turmeric, matcha, and cacao will impart their flavors if you use too much).

To create color using fruit: Puree the fruit, then start by adding ¼ c. to frosting or batter, adding more as you go to adjust the color to your liking. Take care not to make your batter or frosting too runny. You will get some of the flavor of the fruit, but it's worth it considering the beautiful color you'll get.

To create color using vegetables: When using something highly colored like beets or carrots, puree, then start by adding a teaspoon to frosting or batter. Adjust the amount as you go, taking care not to water down your batter or frosting.

Prep Work

Preparing your ingredients ahead of time—doing, in essence, the work of a sous chef—will save you a lot of time and frustration. When you plan to make a recipe, scan the ingredients well ahead of cooking time (even as far in advance as 1 or 2 days if you can) and see what needs to be soaked or melted or otherwise pre-prepped. Here are a few to look out for.

Do ahead to have on hand:

• Make chocolate in large amounts and store in the freezer

• Grind nuts into flour and store it in airtight jars

• Make an ice-cream base, and pour into ice cube trays for storing

Do ahead the day before:

• Soak nuts overnight (see page 29)

• Soak Irish moss for several hours (see page 28)

Do right before making a recipe:

• Melt coconut oil and store in a warm spot

• Melt cacao butter and store in a warm spot

Also note that many of the recipes require placing the dessert in the freezer or refrigerator for a few hours to allow it to set before serving. This is time when you needn't be doing anything, so don't worry, the recipes will not be time-consuming!

TWO

CAKES, PIES, COBBLERS, AND TARTS

MARBELOUS MOCHA FUDGE CAKE

Yield: One 8" round cake
Prep time: 40 minutes, plus about 3 hours for cake to set

CRUST

12 pitted dates

1 c. pecans

½ c. almonds

1 tsp. ground cinnamon

1 tsp. vanilla bean powder or vanilla extract

FILLING

2 c. cashews, soaked and drained (see page 29)

¼ c. cacao powder

1½ c. almond milk

½ c. agave nectar

½ c. coconut butter

½ c. melted coconut oil (see page 28)

¼ c. cold-brewed coffee*

CARAMEL SWIRLS

2 tbsp. lucuma powder

2 tbsp. agave nectar

2 tbsp. melted cacao butter (see page 27)

* Cold-brewed coffee is made from steeping coffee grounds in room temperature or cold water for 12 hours or more, resulting in a coffee concentrate. Many coffee cafes and markets sell cold-brewed coffee or you can make it yourself using coarsely ground beans and a ratio of ⅓ c. coffee to 1½ c. filtered water. Let steep for at least 12 hours, then strain. You can use the leftover for ice coffee.

One summer, Alex and I picked up and took a spontaneous camping trip to Yosemite National Park. Unlike most campers, we decided to bring a freshly made dessert, this Marbelous Mocha Fudge Cake. We packed a cooler full of ice and set out on our adventure, a truly decadent camping trip—I guess you could call it "glamping." Laughing at ourselves as we sat at our campsite eating a cake in the woods, we were also watching our back for bears. Thankfully none appeared, but hiking later on we found a shirt that appeared to have chocolate stains and had been mauled, as if a bear had attacked it. Had we dodged a bullet? Probably—but it made for a memorable trip!

We remind ourselves of our luck every year on Alex's birthday when I make him this cake, his favorite.

To make the crust: Place the dates, pecans, almonds, cinnamon, and vanilla bean powder in a food processor and process until a fine crumble forms and sticks together. Press the crust into the bottom of an 8" round springform pan. Set the crust aside and make the filling.

To make the filling: Place the cashews, cacao powder, almond milk, agave nectar, coconut butter, coconut oil, and cold-brewed coffee in a blender or food processor and process until smooth. Pour the filling on top of the crust and make the caramel swirls.

To make the caramel swirls: In a small bowl, whisk together the lucuma powder, agave nectar, and melted cacao butter until smooth. From a distance of about 6", lightly drizzle the caramel over the cake filling. Using a toothpick, wooden skewer, or tip of a slim knife, gently swirl the caramel to create a marbled pattern. Be mindful not to stick your tool in too deep; you want to keep the caramel swirls on top.

Place the cake in the freezer for 3 hours or until completely firm. Serve immediately or store in the refrigerator for up to 3 days.

♥ MAKE IT YOUR OWN ♥

TRIPLE-LAYER GERMAN CHOCOLATE CAKE

Yield: One 4½" cake

Prep time: 45 minutes, plus about 3 hours for frosting to set

CHOCOLATE CREAM FROSTING

2 c. chilled coconut cream

1 c. cacao powder

½ c. coconut nectar

1 tsp. vanilla bean powder or vanilla extract

PECAN AND COCONUT TOPPING

1 c. pecans

1 c. finely shredded unsweetened coconut

1 tsp. vanilla bean powder or vanilla extract

⅛ tsp. fine sea salt

3 tbsp. coconut nectar

CAKE LAYERS

1 c. coconut flour

1½ c. almond flour

1 tsp. vanilla bean powder or vanilla extract

1½ c. cacao powder

¾ c. coconut nectar

2 tbsp. almond butter

This recipe is a homage to my dear German friend Christiane, who loves dark, rich chocolate as much as I do. When I travel abroad I often bring her chocolate and she does the same for me. Given her European taste buds, she's made a great taste tester for many of the chocolate recipes in this book. And lucky for me, Christiane, who is also my photographer, willingly accepts payment in the form of chocolate.

....

To make the frosting: Place the coconut cream, cacao powder, coconut nectar, and vanilla bean powder in a medium bowl and whisk thoroughly. Refrigerate until firm, about 3 hours. Meanwhile, make the topping and cake layers.

To make the topping: Place the pecans, unsweetened coconut, vanilla bean powder, sea salt, and coconut nectar in a food processor. Process until the crumbs stick together lightly when you pinch the mixture between your fingers. You are looking for a fluffy texture, so do not overprocess. Set aside and make the cake layers.

To make the cake layers: Place the coconut flour, almond flour, vanilla bean powder, cacao powder, coconut nectar, and almond butter in a food processor and process until a fine flour begins to stick slightly together.

Line a 4½" springform pan with enough plastic wrap to come up over the sides and press one-third of the cake layer mixture into the pan. Once you have evenly pressed the mixture into the pan, gently lift up on the plastic wrap and transfer the cake layer to a plate. Repeat this process two more times. Wrap each cake layer individually in the plastic wrap and allow to firm up in the refrigerator while the frosting is firming.

To assemble: Once the frosting has thickened, remove the cake layers from the refrigerator. Place one cake layer on a plate and frost completely with an offset spatula. Sprinkle one-third of the pecan and coconut topping on top of the first frosted layer, then top with the second layer. Repeat until all the layers have been added and the cake is completely frosted all the way around. Use any remaining frosting to pipe around the edges for a pretty finish or refrigerate for use with another recipe. Top the cake with the remaining pecan and coconut topping. Serve immediately or store in the refrigerator for up to 2 days.

♥ MAKE IT YOUR OWN ♥

CHOCOLATE ALMOND HAZELNUT CARAMEL APPLE TORTE

Yield: One 9" cake
Prep time: 40 minutes

This chocolaty, caramel-y cake is the perfect recipe to serve a crowd. As long as you're making the caramel, you might as well make extra and store it in the refrigerator. It's great to have on hand for making anything, even store-bought goodies and ice cream, taste homemade.

Line a 9" cake pan with parchment paper.

To make the cake: Place the almond flour, cacao powder, coconut palm sugar, and vanilla bean in the bowl of an electric mixer. Mix on medium speed for 30 seconds. Add the almond butter and mix again until combined. Add the dates and almond milk and mix again for 30 seconds. (This cake can also be made in a food processor but be careful not to overpulse.)

Pour the mixture into the cake pan and press with your fingers to make a flat bottom layer approximately ½" thick. Continue pressing the mixture about ¼" up the sides of the pan. Set aside and make the caramel.

To make the caramel sauce: Place the melted cacao butter into a small bowl and add the coconut nectar, lucuma powder, and butterscotch extract. Whisk with a fork until all clumps are gone and the mixture turns a caramel color. If necessary, to keep the sauce fluid, transfer to (or leave in) a heatproof bowl and place over a pot of simmering water (or use a double boiler). Drizzle three-fourths of the caramel over the torte crust, and reserve the remainder for garnish. Set aside and make the apple filling.

To make the apple filling: Place the apples, coconut crystals, and lemon juice in a medium bowl and stir until well combined. Arrange the chopped apples over the caramel and top with the raw chocolate and hazelnut toppings. Make the chocolate sauce.

To make the chocolate sauce: In a small bowl, whisk the cacao powder, vanilla bean powder, and coconut nectar together. Drizzle over the cake. Drizzle the remaining caramel over the torte. Serve immediately or store in the refrigerator for up to 3 days.

CAKE

3 c. almond flour

½ c. cacao powder

6 tbsp. coconut palm sugar

4" piece vanilla bean

¼ c. almond butter

20 pitted khadrawi dates or 12 medjools

¼ c. almond milk

CARAMEL SAUCE

¾ c. plus 2 tbsp. melted cacao butter (see page 27)

¾ c. coconut nectar

¼ c. lucuma powder

1 tsp. butterscotch extract

APPLE FILLING

3 red apples, such as Fuji, cored and cubed

2 tbsp. coconut crystals

Juice of 1 lemon

TOPPINGS

1 c. melted raw chocolate (page 32)

½ c. chopped hazelnuts

CHOCOLATE SAUCE

¼ c. cacao powder

½ tsp. vanilla bean powder or vanilla extract

¼ c. coconut nectar

PEACHBERRY LAYER CAKE WITH VANILLA-HONEY FROSTING

Yield: Approximately 4½" cake
Prep time: 30 minutes

CAKE LAYERS

12 pitted medjool dates
¾ c. almond flour
½ c. coconut flour
1 tsp. vanilla extract

FRUIT FILLING

1 white peach, pitted and chopped
½ c. blueberries
Pinch of ground cardamom
3 tbsp. coconut nectar

VANILLA-HONEY FROSTING

3 stems fresh lavender
2 c. chilled coconut cream
2 tbsp. buckwheat or other honey
1 tsp. vanilla extract

All winter long I dream of peaches, and when they first begin appearing at the farmers' market, I'm in heaven. The only trouble with peaches is that you have to watch them carefully. I line them up on my counter to soften, but look away for too long and they turn moldy. Peaches are a seize-the-day fruit: putting them in the refrigerator ruins the flavor and texture, so you've got to use them right when they ripen. I'm partial to white peaches, which are called for here, but you can use yellow varieties—or even nectarines if you like.

This cake features three alternative sweeteners—coconut nectar, honey, and dates—all of which are a far sight healthier than the refined, nutritionally void white stuff.

To make the cake layers: Place the dates, almond flour, coconut flour, and vanilla extract in a food processor and process until they achieve a flourlike consistency. Line a small glass bowl with parchment paper.

Fill the bowl with half the mixture and press it down with your fingers until it forms a round cake layer. Remove the molded cake layer from the bowl, set it aside, and repeat the process for the second layer. Set aside and make the fruit filling.

To make the fruit filling: Place the peach, blueberries, cardamom, and coconut nectar in a small mixing bowl and gently stir to combine. Set aside and make the frosting.

To make the frosting: Place the lavender, coconut cream, honey, and vanilla extract in a medium mixing bowl and gently stir to combine. Set aside.

To assemble: Place one of the cake layers on a cake plate. Spread one-third of the frosting on top. Spread half the fruit over the frosting. Place the second cake layer on top, and repeat. Use the remaining frosting to ice the top and sides of the cake. Refrigerate for 1 hour before serving. Serve immediately or store in the refrigerator for up to 2 days.

♥ SUBSTITUTIONS ♥

You can use any fruit you'd like with this cake. I like peaches for their soft and juicy qualities, but you may also enjoy berries or a mix of peaches and berries.

If you're a chocolate lover, try substituting the chocolate frosting on page 44 for the vanilla-honey one here. It will create an entirely different look and taste.

♥ MAKE IT YOUR OWN ♥

STRAWBERRY SUBLIME "CHEESE" CAKE

Yield: One 9" cake

Prep time: 25 minutes, plus 2–4 hours for cake to set

CRUST

1 c. pecans

½ c. almonds

½ c. pistachios

1 tsp. ground cinnamon

FILLING

1 c. melted coconut oil (see page 28)

2¼ c. cashew flour

¾ c. agave nectar

¼ c. lemon juice

1 tsp. vanilla bean powder or vanilla extract

TOPPING

2¼ c. strawberries

2 tbsp. lemon juice

1 tbsp. agave nectar

I call this my nostalgia cake. It's not so much that it makes me nostalgic, but it seems to send everyone else who tries it down memory lane. People say it reminds them of the cake their mom or grandmother or Sara Lee once made. As for me, this cake mostly just reminds me of the Strawberry Shortcake dolls I used to play with. They had a scent very much like this cake—and believe me, they smelled yummy!

To make the crust: Process the pecans, almonds, pistachios, and cinnamon in a food processor until well combined but still very crumbly. Pour the mixture into a 9" springform pan. Working your way from the center out, press the crumbs down and out toward the edges, lining only the bottom of the pan. Set aside and make the filling.

To make the filling: Place the melted coconut oil in a food processor and add the cashew flour, agave nectar, lemon juice, and vanilla bean powder. Process until smooth and creamy. Pour the filling over the crust, then place in the refrigerator and allow the cake to set while you prepare the topping.

··············· ♥ TIPS & TRICKS ♥ ···············

Save money and time trying to locate cashew flour by making your own. Simply place the cashews in a food processor or coffee grinder and process until a fine flour texture is achieved. Do not overprocess or you will get cashew butter, which is delicious but won't quite work for this recipe.

My trick for removing the bitter center (the hull) of a strawberry is to use a small tool called a strawberry huller. It's faster than using a paring knife and it's also a lot of fun to use!

To make the topping: Hull the strawberries and, placing your thumb inside of the hollowed berry, flatten them by pinching your index finger and thumb together. Place the flattened berries in a bowl with the lemon juice and agave nectar and let sit for 5 minutes to allow the strawberries to macerate.

To assemble: Remove the cake from the refrigerator, and top the filling with the strawberries. Place the cake in the freezer for 2 hours or until firm. Serve immediately or store in the refrigerator for up to 5 days or in the freezer for up to 3 months.

♥ SAVOR THIS ♥

Strawberries are a great source of vitamin C, folic acid, and fiber. Just eight berries provide 160 percent of the vitamin C you need for the whole day.

♥ MAKE IT YOUR OWN ♥

MATCHA MINT CHOCOLATE "CHEESE" CAKE

Yield: One 9" round cake
Prep time: 30 minutes, plus 2–4 hours for cake to set

In this recipe, cashews replace a traditional cheesecake base, with matcha and mint supplying the delicate flavoring. What I love most about this cake is that it's seasonless—it's perfect in summer when you want something refreshing, and also festive enough to serve during the holidays.

To make the crust: Place the almonds, cacao powder, hemp seeds, agave nectar, and mint extract in a food processor and process until the mixture sticks together when pressed between your fingers. Press the crust into the bottom of a 9" springform pan. Set aside and make the filling.

To make the filling: Place the cashews, Irish moss, agave nectar, almond milk, coconut oil, coconut butter, matcha powder, and vanilla bean powder in a blender and blend until smooth. Pour the filling over crust and place the cake in the freezer for 2–4 hours. Meanwhile, make the chocolate garnish.

To make the chocolate garnish: In a small bowl, whisk together the cacao butter, cacao powder, agave nectar, and vanilla extract until smooth. Set the bowl in the freezer until the chocolate hardens all the way through.

To assemble: When the cake is firm enough to cut, remove from the freezer. Grate the chocolate garnish on top before serving. Serve immediately or store in the refrigerator for up to 5 days or in the freezer for up to 3 months.

CRUST

2 c. almonds
½ c. cacao powder
¼ c. hemp seeds
¼ c. agave nectar
1 tbsp. mint extract

FILLING

2 c. cashews, soaked and drained (see page 29)
½ oz. Irish moss, soaked and drained (see page 28)
½ c. agave nectar
½ c. almond milk
½ c. melted coconut oil (see page 28)
2 tbsp. coconut butter, softened
2 tsp. matcha powder
1 tsp. vanilla bean powder or vanilla extract

CHOCOLATE GARNISH

¼ c. melted cacao butter (see page 27)
¼ c. cacao powder
3 tbsp. agave nectar
½ tsp. vanilla extract

.... ♥ MAKE IT YOUR OWN ♥ ....

CHOCOLATE-DIPPED STRAWBERRY CAKE

Yield: One 10" cake
Prep time: 1 hour, plus 2–4 hours for cake to set

STRAWBERRY FILLING

2 c. strawberries, hulled

1 tbsp. lemon juice

2 tbsp. agave nectar

CAKE FILLING

1 c. cashews, soaked and drained (see page 29)

½ c. melted coconut oil (see page 28)

1 oz. Irish moss, soaked and drained (see page 28)

¼ c. agave nectar

Juice of 1 lemon

1 tsp. beet extract for color (optional, see page 38)

CRUST

1 c. almonds

¼ c. agave nectar

2 tbsp. cacao powder

1 tsp. vanilla bean powder or vanilla extract

CHOCOLATE SWIRL SAUCE

½ c. coconut nectar

½ c. cacao powder

2 tsp. melted coconut oil (see page 28)

1 tsp. vanilla extract

The chocolate-dipped strawberries that make this cake so stunning can also just be served on their own, so make extra if you like—they're a great chocolate-craving quencher.

To make the strawberry filling: Place the berries in a medium bowl with the lemon juice and agave nectar and stir to coat. Set aside and make the cake filling.

To make the cake filling: Place the cashews, coconut oil, Irish moss, agave nectar, lemon juice, and, if desired, beet extract in a blender and blend until smooth and creamy. Set aside and make the crust.

To make the crust: Place the almonds, agave nectar, cacao powder, and vanilla bean powder in a food processor and process until the mixture sticks together when pressed between your fingertips. Press the crust mixture evenly on the bottom of a 10" springform pan. Pour the cake filling on top of the crust and place in the freezer while preparing the chocolate swirl sauce and the white chocolate–dipped strawberries.

To make the chocolate swirl sauce: Place the coconut nectar, cacao powder, coconut oil, and vanilla extract in a medium bowl and mix well with a fork. Reserve ¼ c. of the chocolate swirl sauce for the white chocolate–dipped strawberries. Remove the cake from the freezer and drizzle the remaining sauce on top of the filling, using a toothpick to swirl the chocolate into the pink strawberry layer. Be sure not to overswirl or the whole cake will turn brown. Make the white chocolate–dipped strawberries.

♥ TIPS & TRICKS ♥

If you're not pressed for time, here's an extra step that can improve this recipe: freeze the berries for about 20 minutes, or until chilled, before dipping. That will enable the chocolate coating to stick better and dry faster. Don't freeze the berries for longer than 20 minutes—you just want them chilled, not frozen.

To make the white chocolate–dipped strawberries: Place the cashews, vanilla extract, agave nectar, and almond milk in a blender and blend until smooth. Add the cacao butter and coconut oil. Blend lightly until well mixed, transfer to a small bowl, and allow to sit for 5 minutes to thicken.

Coat the strawberries with the white chocolate by holding the stem and dipping the berry into the bowl of white chocolate. Dangle the berry over the bowl to allow any excess to drip off, then place the berry on a plate to dry. (You may want to double coat the berry, but only apply the second coat after the first has dried.) Drizzle the reserved ¼ c. of chocolate swirl sauce over the berries and set them in the refrigerator to harden, approximately 10 minutes. Once all the berries have been coated and hardened, arrange them on top of the cake and set in the refrigerator until completely firm, approximately 2–4 hours. Serve immediately or store in the refrigerator for up to 3 days.

WHITE CHOCOLATE FOR DIPPING

½ c. cashews, soaked and drained (see page 29)

½ tsp. vanilla extract

3 tbsp. agave nectar

1 tbsp. almond milk

½ c. melted cacao butter (see page 27)

1½ tsp. melted coconut oil (see page 28)

10 large strawberries

♥ MAKE IT YOUR OWN ♥

MOST FAVORED RASPBERRY MACADAMIA CAKE

Yield: One 8″ round cake
Prep time: 30 minutes, plus about 4 hours for cake to set

The vast majority of my clients and friends have voted this cake as their favorite from my PatisseRaw dessert line. I was never much of a raspberry fan myself, but this cake has truly made a raspberry lover out of me, too. But if raspberries aren't your thing, try substituting blueberries. The richness of the macadamias contrasted with the tart-sweet berries makes it a winner either way.

To make the crust: Place the macadamia nuts, vanilla bean powder, and agave nectar in a food processor and process until the mixture sticks together when pressed between your fingers. Line an 8″ springform pan or round cake pan with plastic wrap and press the crust into the bottom of the pan. Set aside and make the filling.

To make the filling: Place the cashews, coconut oil, agave nectar, lemon juice, and vanilla bean powder in a food processor or blender and blend until smooth and creamy. Add the raspberries to the blender or food processor and process until well combined. Pour the filling on top of the crust and place the pan in the freezer for about 4 hours or until firm. In the meantime, make the chocolate garnish.

To make the chocolate garnish: While the cake is firming up in the freezer, place the cacao butter, cacao powder, agave nectar, and vanilla extract in a small bowl and whisk until smooth. Set the bowl in the freezer until the chocolate hardens all the way through, approximately 20–30 minutes. Remove the cake from the freezer and grate the chocolate on top before serving. Serve immediately or store in the refrigerator for up to 3 days.

CRUST

2 c. macadamia nuts

1 tsp. vanilla bean powder or vanilla extract

¼ c. agave nectar

FILLING

2¼ c. cashews

1 c. melted coconut oil (see page 28)

½ c. agave nectar

Juice of 1 lemon

1 tsp. vanilla bean powder or vanilla extract

1 pint fresh raspberries

CHOCOLATE GARNISH

¼ c. melted cacao butter (see page 27)

¼ c. cacao powder

3 tbsp. agave nectar

½ tsp. vanilla extract

FANCIFUL FRUITCAKE

Yield: One 9" round cake
Prep time: 40 minutes, plus about 3 hours for cake to set

CAKE

2 c. macadamia nuts

8 pitted medjool dates

¼ c. coconut flakes

2 tbsp. lemon balm herb or lemon zest

FILLING

2 c. cashews, soaked and drained (see page 29)

½ c. agave nectar

½ c. almond milk

½ c. melted coconut oil (see page 28)

1 oz. Irish moss, soaked and drained (see page 28)

¼ c. lemon juice

2 tbsp. coconut butter

1 tsp. vanilla bean powder or vanilla extract

FRUIT TOPPING

2 tbsp. blackberries

2 tbsp. raspberries

4 tbsp. sliced strawberries

4 tbsp. blueberries

2 tbsp. lemon juice

2 tbsp. agave nectar

¼ c. peeled and thinly sliced kiwi

¼ c. peeled and thinly sliced or cubed mango

Don't let the term "fruitcake" turn you away from this fresh, rich treat—it's nothing like the typical holiday fruitcake we've all come to know and loathe (or love, depending on your personal preference). Instead of being infused with dried fruit, this cake is topped with fresh mango, kiwi, and a cornucopia of berries. You'll never think of fruitcake the same way again!

To make the cake: Place the macadamia nuts, dates, coconut flakes, and lemon balm herb or zest in a food processor and process until the mixture sticks together when pressed between your fingers. Press the cake into the bottom of a 9" springform pan. Set aside and make the filling.

To make the filling: Place the cashews, agave nectar, almond milk, coconut oil, Irish moss, lemon juice, coconut butter, and vanilla bean powder in a food processor or blender and blend until smooth and creamy. Pour the filling on top of the crust and place in the freezer. Make the fruit topping.

To make the fruit topping: Rinse all berries and place them in a medium bowl. Add the lemon juice and agave nectar and stir to combine. Add the kiwi and mango. Give all the fruit and juices a gentle but thorough stir, cover the bowl, and set in the refrigerator until the cake is firm enough for decorating, about 3 hours. Once the cake is firm, arrange the fruit on the top of the cake in any fashion that you fancy. Serve immediately or store in the refrigerator for up to 3 days.

♥ MAKE IT YOUR OWN ♥

ORANGE MATCHA CREAM CAKE

Yield: One 6" round cake
Prep time: 30 minutes, plus 2–4 hours for cake to set

This is a wonderful cake to make in the winter when citrus is at its peak. Even though oranges are a cold-weather food, they're so refreshing that they make you feel like summer is right around the corner.

To make the bottom layer: Combine the almonds, vanilla bean powder, agave nectar, and orange zest in a food processor and process until the mixture sticks together when pressed between your fingers. Press the mixture into the bottom of a 6" round cake pan. Make the filling.

To make the filling: Place the cashews, Irish moss, matcha powder, vanilla bean powder, agave nectar, coconut oil, almond milk, orange juice, and coconut butter in a blender or food processor and blend until very smooth and creamy. Pour the filling over the crust and set in the freezer until firm, 2–4 hours. Once firm, top with the orange slices. Serve immediately or store in the refrigerator for up to 3 days.

♥ MAKE IT YOUR OWN ♥

BOTTOM CAKE LAYER

1½ c. almonds

1 tsp. vanilla bean powder or vanilla extract

¼ c. agave nectar

2 tbsp. orange zest

FILLING

2 c. cashews, soaked and drained (see page 29)

½ oz. Irish moss, soaked and drained (see page 28)

2 tsp. matcha powder

1 tsp. vanilla bean powder or vanilla extract

½ c. agave nectar

½ c. melted coconut oil (see page 28)

¼ c. almond milk

¼ c. orange juice

2 tbsp. melted coconut butter

6 thin orange slices, for garnish

LEMON BERRY ICEBOX CAKE

Yield: One 9" cake
Prep time: 45 minutes, plus 2–4 hours for cake to set

BOTTOM CAKE LAYER

1 c. pecans
½ c. almonds
¼ c. agave nectar
Zest of ½ lemon

FILLING

1 oz. Irish moss, soaked for 6 hours and drained (see page 28), or 2 tbsp. melted coconut butter
½ c. coconut oil
1 c. cashews, soaked and drained (see page 29)
¼ c. agave nectar
Juice of 4 lemons
1 tsp. vanilla extract

FRUIT SWIRL

15 raspberries
2 tsp. agave nectar
1 tsp. lemon juice

Giving things another chance sometimes has its rewards. I have never really been a fan of lemony desserts, but I saw it as a challenge: maybe I could create something that would captivate even my taste buds. And I did! It's funny how we find inspiration in the most unlikely of places. Be aware as you prepare to make this recipe that if you're using Irish moss, it needs to be soaked for 6 hours.

To make the bottom cake layer: Place the pecans, almonds, agave nectar, and lemon zest in a food processer and process until a crumbly, sticky dough forms. The ingredients must stick together when pinched between your fingers. Press into a 9" cake pan and, working from the outside in, press evenly until a uniform layer is formed. Set aside and make the filling.

To make the filling: Blend the Irish moss (or coconut butter) with the coconut oil in a blender until smooth. Add the cashews, agave nectar, lemon juice, and vanilla extract and blend until smooth. Pour the filling on top of the bottom layer and place in the refrigerator for a few minutes while you make the fruit swirl.

···· ♥ TIPS & TRICKS ♥ ····

To achieve a pretty swirl pattern, you can use a toothpick, lollipop stick, or skewer, or you may even want to use a pointy knife tip. Place whichever tool you choose on the top layer of your cake, no more than ⅛" in to ensure the swirl stays visible. Gently swirl your tool around in any direction or pattern that you choose; as you begin to see a pattern that you like, apply it to other areas. I like to add the fruit puree as I go to ensure I don't oversaturate an area and the swirls remain prominent.

To make the fruit swirl: Blend the raspberries, agave nectar, and lemon juice in a blender until smooth. Strain the seeds using a fine-mesh strainer or fine cheesecloth. Pour the fruit puree on top of the cake slowly and spread it out using a thin wooden stick such as a toothpick, skewer, or knife tip (see opposite for more tips on swirling). Swirl the fruit into a fluid pattern. Place the cake in the freezer until firm, 2–4 hours. Serve immediately or store in the refrigerator for up to 3 days.

♥ MAKE IT YOUR OWN ♥

LEMON GINGER KIWI TART

Yield: One 6″ tart
Prep time: 25 minutes, plus 2–4 hours for tart to set

CRUST

1½ c. almonds

8 pitted medjool dates

1 tsp. lemon zest

½ tsp. peeled and chopped ginger

FILLING

⅔ c. cashews, soaked and drained (see page 29)

2 tbsp. peeled and grated ginger

1 oz. Irish moss, soaked and drained (see page 28)

¼ c. honey

¼ c. melted coconut oil (see page 28)

1 tsp. vanilla extract

Juice of 2 Meyer lemons (regular lemons work here, too)

GARNISH

2 kiwis

1 small strand of orange peel

I like to use tart pans that have a removable bottom, as it makes lifting the dessert out a lot smoother. If your pan does not have a removable bottom, simply line it with plastic wrap (leaving 2–3″ overhang) before adding the crust so that it's easy to lift the tart out without it crumbling.

To make the crust: Place the almonds, dates, lemon zest, and ginger in a food processor and process until the mixture is crumbly and sticks together when pressed between your fingers. Press the crust into a 6″ tart pan, starting with the bottom and working your way up and around the fluted edges. Set aside and make the filling.

To make the filling: Place the cashews, ginger, Irish moss, honey, coconut oil, vanilla extract, and lemon juice in a blender and blend until smooth and creamy. Pour the filling over the crust and set in the refrigerator until firm enough to cut, approximately 2–4 hours.

To make the garnish: Using a sharp paring knife, peel and cut the kiwis into thin slices. Lay the slices on top of one another in a circular pattern on top of the tart. Place the orange peel strand in the center of the tart. Serve immediately or store in the refrigerator for up to 3 days.

♥ MAKE IT YOUR OWN ♥

BANANA-TOFFEE PIE

Yield: One 8" pie
Prep time: 30 minutes

CRUST

½ c. Brazil nut flour
½ c. coconut flour
¼ c. coconut palm sugar
⅛ tsp. sea salt
1 tsp. maple extract
1 tsp. vanilla extract
1 tbsp. coconut nectar

CARAMEL

¾ c. plus 2 tbsp. melted cacao butter (see page 27)
¼ c. lucuma powder
¾ c. coconut nectar
1 tsp. butterscotch extract

FILLING

1 large firm but ripe banana

CREAM

1 tsp. vanilla bean powder or vanilla extract
1¾ c. coconut cream

Basic raw chocolate (page 32), for garnish

Alex and I are in love with Costa Rica. He took me there when we first met (it was my very first trip outside of the United States), so it's a place near and dear to my heart. In Costa Rica, the locals are very warm-hearted and the land is verdant and abundant. As soon as you leave the airport in San José, you begin seeing all kinds of fruit trees, especially bananas. There are banana trees everywhere, including right outside our door in Alajuela, the first place we stayed. I quickly learned that there's nothing like the taste of a fresh-picked banana. It has an almost pineapple undertone.

This Banana-Toffee Pie is my homage to Costa Rica and its lovely banana trees. It contains a variety of natural sweeteners, including lucuma powder, a low-glycemic extract from the Peruvian fruit lucuma.

Line an 8" pie pan with wax paper.

To make the crust: Place the Brazil nut flour, coconut flour, palm sugar, sea salt, maple extract, and vanilla extract in a food processor. Turn on the machine and, as it's running, add the coconut nectar. Process until well combined but still very crumbly. Pour the crumbs into the pie pan. Working your way from the center out, press the crumbs down and out toward the edges, then up the sides with your thumb to form an even crust. Set aside and make the caramel.

To make the caramel: Place the melted cacao butter in a small bowl, then add the lucuma powder, coconut nectar, and butterscotch extract. Whisk with a fork until all clumps are gone and the mixture turns a caramel color. Pour three-fourths of the caramel into the piecrust and reserve the remainder for later use. Make the filling and the cream.

To make the filling: Slice the banana into ¼" rounds. Place the slices on top of the caramel layer, working your way from the center out.

To make the cream: Place the vanilla bean powder and coconut cream in a medium bowl. Mix lightly with an electric or hand mixer until fluffy, about 2 minutes.

To assemble: Place a pastry bag in a tall glass, allowing the edges of the bag to hang over the rim of the glass. Scoop the cream into the bag, then use it to create light, interlocking puffs of cream on top of the bananas. Grate just enough raw chocolate over the cream to create a freckling of chocolate. Dip a fork into the remaining caramel and drizzle it lightly on top. Serve immediately or store in the refrigerator for up to 2 days.

♥ PEELING BACK THE MYSTERIES OF BANANAS ♥

Bananas are ubiquitous, but few of us really know more about them than the fact that they soften and sweeten as they ripen. I was fascinated to learn that, as the banana develops, the peel acts as a housing for the chlorophyll manufactured as a result of the direct sunlight. As the interior fruit reaches peak condition, the green peel that had been absorbing all that sunlight begins to release nutrients that mellow the fruit and enhance its sweetness.

At the same time, the peel begins to lose chlorophyll content and changes from green to yellow. During this transformation, the peel itself begins to deteriorate, leaving behind only a thin covering that can be peeled away from the mature fruit with ease. Since bananas ripen quickly, it doesn't take long for one to go from bitter green to sweet and yellow. Depending on the recipe you're making you may choose a banana at various stages in its maturity. For this recipe I prefer one that is still firm and has a fully yellow peel with few brown spots.

I love bananas not only for their tropical flavor but also because they offer a mood boost. And before you throw away that peel, did you know it's a great beauty aid? Applying the inside of the peel to blemishes is a natural way to dry them out.

♥ MAKE IT YOUR OWN ♥

SWEETLY SOUTHERN PECAN PIE SQUARES

Yield: One 8x8" square
Prep time: 30 minutes

CRUST

1 c. cashew flour
1 tbsp. coconut crystals
1 tbsp. lucuma powder
1 tsp. ground cinnamon
1 tsp. vanilla bean powder or vanilla extract
2 tbsp. honey
1 tsp. vanilla extract

TOPPING

1 c. pecans
3 tbsp. coconut nectar or maple syrup
1 tsp. maple extract or maple syrup
1 tsp. vanilla extract

FILLING

24 pitted dates
1 tsp. vanilla bean powder or vanilla extract
2–4 tbsp. filtered water
1 tsp. maple extract or maple syrup

Coconut nectar, for garnish (optional)

My dear mother, Anna Maria Perrone, was born and raised in Italy and by default happens to be a really good "mama" cook. You know, the ones with the big hips (sorry, Mom, but this is a sign of a woman who eats as well as she cooks) who are always waving a wooden spoon? That's my mom. As a result, I'm a lucky girl. She always cooked for me, my three sisters, and my dad, Italian food mostly, but some really wonderful simple American dishes, too.

Holiday time, in particular, was nirvana. Like all kids, my sisters and I would get excited around the holidays, anticipating a lot of gift unwrapping on Christmas morning. But the joy that filled our home during those days was just as much (if not more) due to what was going on in the kitchen. Every holiday season, my mother, sisters, and I spent hours baking cookies, pies, and cakes to go with the well-planned Italian-American lunch and dinner menus my mother was famous for. We'd be in the kitchen working (with them doing most of the work since I wasn't much of a cook in those days) while my dad would be in the living room, cranking up CDs to cheer us on.

One of my mom's best desserts was the classic pecan pie. With memories of my family's Christmas baking traditions dancing in my head, I recreated it to raw/vegan specifications one cold winter's day, working it into a square pan instead of a pie plate. While it's certainly festive enough for the holidays, it's also a wonderful treat any time of year.

♥ MAKE IT YOUR OWN ♥

Line an 8x8″ square pan with parchment paper.

To make the crust: Place the cashew flour, coconut crystals, lucuma powder, cinnamon, vanilla bean powder, honey, and vanilla extract in a food processor and process until the mixture sticks together when pressed between your fingers. Press the crust into the bottom of the square pan, approximately ¼″ thick. Set aside and make the topping.

To make the topping: In a small mixing bowl, combine the pecans, coconut nectar, maple extract, and vanilla extract. Stir gently until the pecans are well coated. Set aside and make the filling.

To make the filling: In a food processor, combine the dates, vanilla bean powder, 2 tbsp. of the water, and maple extract and process until a gooey paste forms, adding more water as needed.

To assemble: Using a spatula, spread the filling evenly over the pressed crust. Spread the topping over the filling until the whole top is covered. If desired, lightly drizzle coconut nectar over the top for a nice finished glaze. Serve immediately or store in the refrigerator for up to 3 days.

SUMMER SUNDAY COBBLER

Yield: One 8" cobbler
Prep time: 10 minutes

CRUMBLE

1 c. pecans

½ c. coconut flour

2 tbsp. coconut nectar

FILLING

3 pluots or plums

3 peaches (preferably a mix of white and yellow)

1 tsp. coconut nectar, for garnish

I dreamed of making cobblers using fresh-picked fruit from my backyard, so I couldn't wait for my loquats and mulberries to ripen, hoping the birds and squirrels didn't devour more than their fair share of my backyard bounty, as they were known to do.

When I returned from a trip, I was happy to see the trees full of perfectly ripened fruit ready for harvesting. But I was also perplexed. Why hadn't all the birds, animals, and insects that frequent the property eaten from the trees? Still, I picked swiftly just in case an island scrub-jay decided to swoop down for dinner. Later on I spotted an unfamiliar cat in the yard—aha! Uneaten fruit mystery solved.

Since loquats and mulberries aren't easy to come by, I've substituted pluots (or plums) and peaches in this recipe, but you can use any fruit you like—apples, pears, cherries, and berries are some of my other favorites. All the better if the fruit comes from your backyard.

To make the crumble: Place the pecans, coconut flour, and coconut nectar in a food processor. Process until crumbly and the mixture sticks lightly together when you press it between your fingers. Set aside and make the filling.

To make the filling: Chop the pluots (or plums) and peaches into bite-size cubes, then place in an 8" glass pie pan.

To assemble: Scatter the crumble over the fruit, then drizzle the crumble top with the coconut nectar. Serve immediately or store in the refrigerator for up to 3 days.

♥ MAKE IT YOUR OWN ♥

♥ TIPS & TRICKS ♥

To serve this cobbler in the winter, place it in a dehydrator or in your oven on the lowest setting just until the dish is warmed. You may even want to add vanilla ice cream or vanilla coconut cream for a garnish when a little extra gourmet decadence is required.

♥ SAVOR THIS ♥

What are pluots? A plum and an apricot fall in love. The result: a delicious blend of juicy plum and apricot goodness. Pluots, sometimes called "dinosaur eggs," usually resemble the plum more than the apricot (even though the apricot likes to think that the pluot looks more like him). Regardless, it's a sweet little fruit with great genes, gorgeous baby-smooth skin, and lots of vitamins A and C. I usually find this summer fruit at the farmers' market or grocery store.

APPLE STREUSEL

Yield: One 9″ streusel
Prep time: 40 minutes

FILLING

3 Fuji or other slightly tart apples, cored

1 tbsp. coconut sugar

1 tsp. ground cinnamon

Juice of ½ lemon

CRUST

1 c. almonds

1 c. pecans

6 large moist, pitted medjool dates

CREAM

1 c. cashews, soaked and drained (see page 29)

1 oz. Irish moss, soaked and drained (see page 28), or 2 tbsp. melted coconut butter

½ tsp. vanilla bean powder or vanilla extract

¼ tsp. ground cloves

¼ c. agave nectar

¼ c. filtered water

½ tsp. ground cinnamon, for garnish

¼ c. chopped pecans, for garnish (optional)

When winter rolls around it's nice to have a warm treat on hand to serve to visitors or to eat yourself (while snuggled up on the couch with a good book and blanket). I developed this recipe one cold winter's day (even Venice Beach gets cold once in a while!) after I was invited to teach a holiday dessert class at Whole Foods. I opted for some familiar wintertime flavors, putting a raw/vegan spin on the traditional dessert.

To make the filling: Using a mandoline or a sharp knife, shave the apples into ⅛" slices. Place the apples, coconut sugar, cinnamon, and lemon juice in a medium bowl. Mix gently using your hands, then cover with a lid. Let the mixture macerate while you prepare the crust.

To make the crust: Using a food processor, process the almonds and pecans finely until they are the consistency of flour. Add the dates and process until the mixture just sticks together when you press it between your fingers. Press half of the mixture into the bottom of a 9" pie pan. Set the other half aside to use for the top layer. Make the cream.

To make the cream: Place the cashews, Irish moss, vanilla bean powder, cloves, agave nectar, and water in a blender and blend until creamy and fluffy.

To assemble: Pour the cream over the crust, reserving 1 tbsp. for garnish. Arrange the apple filling on top of the cream, then pour the remaining juice from the bowl over the apples. Place the remaining crust mixture on top of the apples and pat gently to set. Finish with a dollop of cream on top and sprinkle with the cinnamon and, if desired, pecan pieces. Serve immediately or store in the refrigerator for up to 2 days.

········· ♥ TIPS & TRICKS ♥ ·········

Warm this dish up in your oven for about 5 minutes at 350°F. Or if you have a dehydrator, simply place a slice inside for 10 minutes before serving. During warmer seasons, I set this streusel on the counter for 3–5 minutes before eating. Regardless of how you choose to warm it up, add a scoop of vanilla ice cream for contrasting temperature and texture.

········· ♥ MAKE IT YOUR OWN ♥ ·········

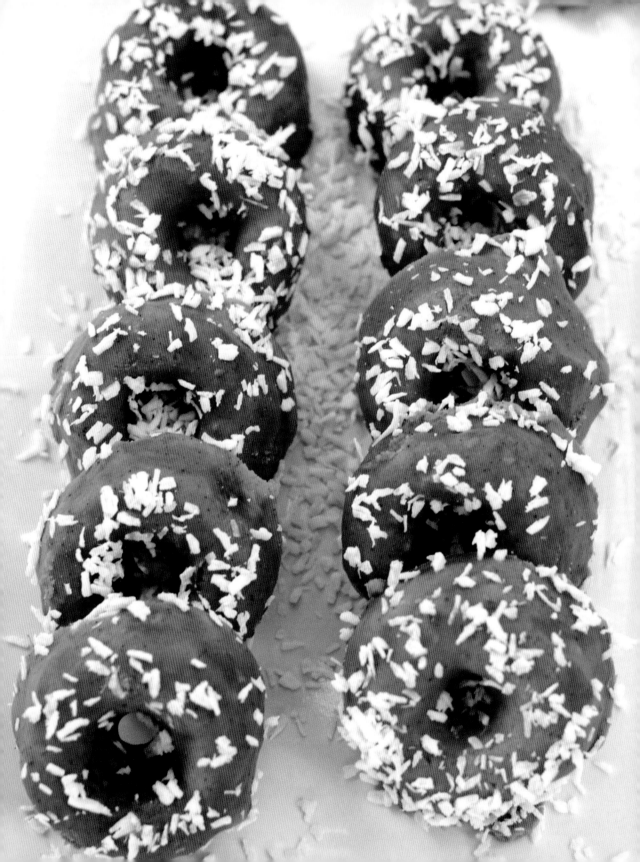

THREE

MINIS AND MORE

MINI MINT CHOCOLATE BROWNIES

Yield: 49 mini brownies

Prep time: 20 minutes, plus 30 minutes for brownies to set

BASE

3 c. pecans

¼ c. cacao powder

¼ c. agave nectar

2 tbsp. almond butter

TOPPING

2 tbsp. cacao powder

½ c. melted cacao butter
(see page 27)

2 tbsp. agave nectar

1 tsp. mint extract

A local coffee shop wanted me to create some desserts for their new display case. Chocolate instantly came to mind. I then began to think about masking the customers' coffee breath with a subtle hint of mint (most coffee spots have peppermints at the register for that very reason). What could be better than combining the two? These brownies became a hit, and I started experimenting with them in a variety of flavors. I hope you'll do the same.

Line a 9x9″ square pan with parchment paper.

To make the base: Place the pecans, cacao powder, agave nectar, and almond butter in a food processor and process until the dough forms a ball. Press the dough into the parchment paper–lined pan. Set aside and make the topping.

To make the topping: Combine the cacao powder, cacao butter, agave nectar, and mint extract in a small bowl and stir with a fork or whisk until all clumps are smoothed out.

To assemble: Pour the topping over the base until it covers the entire pan. Refrigerate for 30 minutes or until the topping hardens. Cut the brownies into a 7x7 grid to make 49 mini brownies. Serve immediately or store covered in a cool, dry place for up to 3 days.

··········· ♥ TIPS & TRICKS ♥ ···········

To make other brownie flavors, exchange the mint extract for other extracts like vanilla or almond. If you like, to customize the base, you can also replace the pecans with other nuts, such as walnuts. Chocolate really goes with everything, so I urge you to experiment.

SPLENDID DAY RED VELVET CUPCAKES

Yield: 12 mini cupcakes (or 6 large)
Prep time: 40 minutes

CUPCAKE BASE

1 tsp. chia seeds

¼ c. almond milk

1 c. almond flour

1 c. coconut flour

⅓ c. coconut crystals

3 tbsp. cacao powder

¼ tsp. sea salt

½ c. plus 2 tbsp. coconut nectar

1 tbsp. beet extract

½ tsp. vanilla bean power or vanilla extract

FROSTING

¼ tsp. vanilla bean powder or vanilla extract

2 c. coconut cream

2 tbsp. agave inulin (optional)

1 tbsp. Meyer lemon juice (regular lemon juice works, too)

Since the cupcake craze shows little sign of slowing down, I made it my mission to develop a raw, vegan version. I first made these as a birthday gift to myself, using, among other ingredients, beet extract instead of food coloring. I should tell you that I am not usually one to celebrate my birthday. I believe in celebrating every day of this life and consider each day to be a gift. So when my birthday rolls around it's just another magical day. Still, as long as I was experimenting in the kitchen, why not create something festive? Don't wait until your birthday to make them!

Line a 12-cup mini cupcake pan or a 6-cup standard cupcake pan with cupcake liners or grease lightly with coconut oil.

To make the cupcake base: In a medium bowl, stir together the chia seeds and almond milk. Let sit for 20 minutes to create a gel.

In a large mixing bowl or the bowl of an electric mixer, combine the almond flour, coconut flour, coconut crystals, cacao powder, and sea salt. Beat with a spoon or the whisk attachment of the mixer for 30 seconds or until all clumps have dissolved.

Add the coconut nectar, beet extract, and vanilla bean powder or extract to the chia gel. Whisk to combine.

Make a well in the center of the dry ingredients and stir in the wet ingredients. Beat for 40 seconds or until clumps begin to form and the mixture shows signs of sticking lightly together.

Using an ice-cream scoop, scoop batter into 12 small or 6 large cupcake liners, filling each to the top and molding the batter into a dome. Set the cupcakes aside and make the frosting.

To make the frosting: Place the vanilla bean powder, coconut cream, agave inulin (if desired), and lemon juice in a chilled mixing bowl or stand mixer with the whisk attachment. Beat for 20 seconds or until well whipped. Do not overmix or the frosting will turn runny.

To assemble: Place a pastry bag in a tall glass, allowing the edges of the bag to hang over the rim of the glass. Scoop the frosting into the bag and use immediately to frost the cupcakes. Alternatively, use a spatula to spread frosting on the cupcakes. Serve immediately. Store any leftover cupcakes in the refrigerator.

♥ SAVOR THIS ♥

Agave inulin is a powdered form of agave sweetener. It's a nice substitute for granulated and powdered white sugar and actually contains fiber, something agave syrup (not to mention white sugar) doesn't have. Agave inulin is also easy on blood sugar levels—it won't set you up for a big boost and subsequent crash.

♥ MAKE IT YOUR OWN ♥

CARROT COLLECTIVE CUPCAKES

Yield: 24 mini cupcakes
Prep time: 25 minutes, plus about 2 hours for frosting to set

CUPCAKE BASE

4 c. shredded carrot (approximately 8 carrots)

2 c. pecans

2 c. raisins

1 c. shredded coconut

¼ c. hemp seeds

2 tsp. agave nectar

4 tsp. almond oil

FROSTING

½ c. cashews

½ c. macadamia nuts

1 c. coconut milk

½ c. melted coconut butter

¼ c. agave nectar

1 tbsp. vanilla extract

1 tbsp. lemon juice

24 whole pecans, for garnish

Ground cinnamon, for garnish

Carrot cake without cream cheese frosting? Some people might say that's heresy, but we know better, don't we? For these cupcakes, I created a frosting with the sweetness of coconut milk and the tang of lemon. They're the most delicious way I know to get in a good dose of (carrot-delivered) beta-carotene.

Line two 12-cup mini cupcake pans with cupcake liners or grease lightly with coconut oil.

To make the cupcake base: Begin by pulsing the carrots in a food processor until pulpy. Add the pecans and raisins and pulse until roughly chopped and combined with the carrots. Add the shredded coconut, hemp seeds, agave nectar, and almond oil and pulse until the mixture holds together. Divide the mixture among the 24 cupcake liners, pressing the dough into the pan. Refrigerate while you make the frosting.

To make the frosting: Place the cashews, macadamia nuts, coconut milk, coconut butter, agave nectar, vanilla extract, and lemon juice in a blender and blend until smooth. Pour into a medium bowl, cover, and place in the refrigerator until firm enough to scoop, about 2 hours.

To assemble: Using an offset spatula, gently remove the cupcakes from the pan. Frost the cupcakes, then garnish each with a whole pecan and a sprinkling of cinnamon. Serve immediately or store in the refrigerator for up to 2 days.

♥ MAKE IT YOUR OWN ♥

STRAWBERRY BABYCAKES

Yield: 9 babycakes
Prep time: 25 minutes, plus 20 minutes for cake to set

BERRY TOPPING
Juice of ½ lemon
2 tsp. honey
8 large strawberries, hulled
1½ tsp. chia seeds

BABYCAKES
1 c. cashews
¼ c. almonds
½ tsp. vanilla bean powder or vanilla extract
2 tbsp. honey
2 tsp. almond extract

Mint leaves, for garnish (optional)

This is the raw answer to strawberry shortcake. The strawberry topping is thickened with chia seed gel, which adds a little extra fiber, protein, and omega-3s to the mix.

To make the berry topping: In a medium bowl, whisk together the lemon juice and honey. Add the strawberries and allow to soak for 10 minutes. Mash the strawberries with the back of a fork, then stir in the chia seeds. Allow to sit for 10 minutes to thicken. Strain the berry mixture to separate the fruit from the juice. Discard the juice and set the fruit aside. Make the babycakes.

To make the babycakes: Place the cashews and almonds in a food processor and process into a fine flour. Add the vanilla bean powder, honey, and almond extract. Process until the mixture sticks together when pressed between your fingers.

To assemble: Using an ice-cream scoop, form the dough into 9 balls and make a depression in the center with your thumb or the back of a spoon. Refrigerate for 20 minutes to firm. Fill with the strawberry topping. Garnish with mint leaves, if desired, and serve immediately or store in the refrigerator for up to 3 days.

♥ MAKE IT YOUR OWN ♥

BIG BANG BROWNIE CUPCAKES

Yield: 14 cupcakes

Prep time: 15 minutes, plus about 1 hour for frosting to set

FROSTING

2 c. cashews

2 tsp. vanilla bean powder or vanilla extract

½ c. filtered water

¼ c. coconut nectar

2 tbsp. coconut oil

CUPCAKE BASE

3 c. pecans

¼ c. cacao powder

¼ c. coconut nectar

2 tbsp. almond butter

Sliced almonds, for garnish

Cacao powder, for garnish

Surprisingly, my love affair with chocolate started with white chocolate. When I was a young girl, nothing else would do. Eventually, though, the Cadbury Easter egg crossed my path, and I fell in love with milk chocolate with a sugary filling. Further down the line, I began an affair with dark chocolate until, finally, I found pure cacao. It was love at first bite.

Perhaps, though, I've taken my love affair with chocolate a tad bit too far. The other day when wandering around the grocery store, I gave in and bought copious amounts of chocolate—even though I already had tons at home. But I couldn't resist! The colorful packages with labels touting delicious combinations like chocolate with orange hibiscus, chocolate with ginger and almond—really, why would I deprive myself of these pleasures?

If you, too, have an intense relationship with chocolate, you're going to fall hard for these cupcakes. They're slightly chewier than traditional cupcakes, but the richness makes up for it.

Line 2 cupcake pans with 14 liners or grease lightly with coconut oil.

To make the frosting: Place the cashews in a food processor and process into a fine flour. Add the vanilla bean powder, water, coconut nectar, and coconut oil and process until smooth. Pour the creamy liquid into an airtight container and place in the refrigerator to firm up, about 1 hour. In the meantime, make the cupcake base.

To make the cupcake base: Place the pecans in a food processor and process until they attain a fluffy texture and flourlike consistency. Give it a good stir by hand, then add the cacao powder, coconut nectar, and almond butter. Continue to process until the mixture forms a solid ball. Transfer to a medium bowl and give the dough a good stir by hand to make sure it is mixed well.

Using an ice-cream scoop, scoop the brownie base into the cupcake liners. Press the mixture into the cups and set in the refrigerator for 30 minutes or until firm.

To assemble: Remove the cupcakes from the pan. Frost with an offset spatula, then garnish with sliced almonds and a sprinkle of cacao powder. Serve immediately or store in the refrigerator for up to 2 days.

♥ TIPS & TRICKS ♥

- For an even richer frosting, replace the water with your favorite nut milk.

- For a simpler (and very pretty) way to serve these, instead of making the frosting, press your thumb into the center of the cupcake base and place a berry in the indentation.

♥ MAKE IT YOUR OWN ♥

MINI CINNY ROLLS

Yield: 8 mini rolls
Prep time: 30 minutes

GLAZE

1 c. cashews, soaked and drained (see page 29)

1 oz. Irish moss, soaked and drained (see page 28)

1 tsp. vanilla bean powder or vanilla extract

½ tsp. ground cloves

¼ c. filtered water

¼ c. agave nectar

DOUGH

1 c. almond flour

½ c. raisins

2 tsp. ground cinnamon

½ tsp. ground cardamom

½ tsp. ground nutmeg

3 tbsp. maple syrup

2 tsp. orange blossom water

Flax meal, for rolling

FILLING

15 pitted medjool dates

½ tsp. vanilla bean powder or vanilla extract

2 tbsp. filtered water

Cinnamon rolls, and I'm talking about those giant rolls sold in conventional bakeries, should be called sinnamon rolls—they're that wicked. These mini cinny rolls, on the other hand, are filled with healthy-for-you stuff like cashews, almond flour, and dates. Nonetheless, they still have that spicy, gooey goodness that makes cinnamon rolls so addictive. Enjoy without the guilt!

To make the glaze: Place the cashews, Irish moss, vanilla bean powder, ground cloves, water, and agave nectar in a blender and blend until smooth. Set aside and make the dough.

To make the dough: Place the almond flour, raisins, cinnamon, cardamom, nutmeg, maple syrup, and orange blossom water in a food processor and process until the dough forms a ball.

Sprinkle flax meal on a cutting board. Divide the dough into 2 balls. Flatten each ball on the cutting board either by hand or using a rolling pin, and shape into a 3x8" rectangle about ¼" thick. Cut off uneven edges. Set aside and make the filling.

To make the filling: Place the dates, vanilla bean powder, and water in a food processor and process until the mixture forms a paste.

To assemble: Spread the filling evenly over the 2 dough rectangles. Roll each rectangle into a log, applying gentle pressure. Cut the rolls into eight 1" pieces. Place on a serving platter and pour the glaze over the rolls. Serve the rolls immediately or let them firm up in the refrigerator. If you like a warm, gooey cinnamon bun, dehydrate them for approximately 30 minutes in a 108°F oven. Store leftover cinnamon rolls in the refrigerator for up to 3 days.

♥ MAKE IT YOUR OWN ♥

WHITE CHOCOLATE MACADAMIA POPS

Yield: 12 pops
Prep time: 15 minutes, plus 10 minutes for pops to set

POP DOUGH

1 c. macadamia nuts

4 pitted medjool dates

2 tbsp. coconut flakes

½ tsp. vanilla bean powder

WHITE CHOCOLATE

½ c. cashews, soaked and drained (see page 29)

½ tsp. vanilla extract

3 tbsp. agave nectar

1 tbsp. almond milk

½ c. melted cacao butter (see page 27)

1½ tsp. melted coconut oil (see page 28)

12 Popsicle or other wooden sticks

This recipe came about when I was creating a crust for a cheese-cake. I sampled these ingredients together and fell so in love with the combination that I knew it had to be a stand-alone recipe. Keeping things simple, I decided to make these pops. I love using colorful Popsicle sticks, but lollipop sticks will also work well here.

To make the pop dough: Combine the macadamia nuts, dates, coconut flakes, and vanilla bean powder in a food processor. Process until smooth and dough-like. Form the mixture into twelve 1" balls using a melon baller or by rolling between your hands. Place the balls on a plate and store in the refrigerator while you make the white chocolate.

To make the white chocolate: Place the cashews, vanilla extract, agave nectar, and almond milk in a blender and blend until smooth. Add the cacao butter and coconut oil. Blend lightly until well mixed. Allow to sit for 5 minutes to thicken.

To assemble: While the white chocolate is thickening, insert wooden sticks into the dough balls. Gently push the stick half to three-quarters of the way through the ball. Dip the ball into the white chocolate and twirl the stick around to remove excess chocolate. Stand the pop up in a cup or push the stick into an apple to hold the pop upright while you continue to dip the others. Place the pops in the refrigerator for 10 minutes or until the chocolate has dried. Serve immediately or store in the refrigerator for up to 3 days.

♥ MAKE IT YOUR OWN ♥

LEMON POPPY ALMOND CREAM TARTLETS

Yield: Three 4" tartlets
Prep time: 30 minutes, plus 2 hours for filling to set

CRUST

1 c. almonds

⅔ c. dried figs (approximately 10)

1 tsp. vanilla bean powder or vanilla extract

⅛ tsp. sea salt

1 tbsp. coconut nectar

FILLING

1½ c. cashews, soaked and drained (see page 29)

⅛ tsp. sea salt

¼ tsp. turmeric

¼ tsp. vanilla bean powder or vanilla extract

¼ c. lemon juice (approximately 3 small lemons)

¼ c. coconut oil

¼ c. filtered water

1½ tbsp. honey

1 tsp. almond extract

1 tbsp. poppy seeds, for garnish

3 mint leaves, for garnish

These little tartlets are the perfect combination of tart and sweet. If you don't have small tartlet pans, large cupcake liners placed into ramekins or cupcake molds work as a perfect substitute.

Line three 4" tartlet pans with plastic wrap, allowing 1–2" of wrap to hang over the sides.

To make the crust: Place the almonds, dried figs, vanilla bean powder, sea salt, and coconut nectar in a food processor and process until crumbly and the mixture sticks together when you press it between your fingers. Divide the crust among the 3 pans. Press the dough down from the center out to form the crust, and flute the edges as you mold it into the pan. Place the crusts in the freezer to firm up while you make the filling.

To make the filling: Place the cashews, sea salt, turmeric, vanilla bean powder, lemon juice, coconut oil, water, honey, and almond extract in a blender and blend until smooth and creamy. Pour the mixture into a bowl, cover, and refrigerate until well chilled, about 2 hours.

To assemble: Lift the crusts from their pans by pulling up on the plastic wrap. Remove the plastic wrap and gently place the crusts on a platter. Gently spoon the filling into the three crusts and smooth with a spatula. Garnish each tartlet with 1 tsp. poppy seeds and 1 mint leaf. Serve immediately or store in the refrigerator for up to 3 days.

♥ MAKE IT YOUR OWN ♥

MANGO SUNRISE SURPRISE "CHEESE" CAKE BITES

Yield: 49 cake bites
Prep time: 40 minutes, plus 2–4 hours for cake to set

CRUST

½ c. pecans

½ c. almonds

½ c. Brazil nuts

½ c. dried cranberries

¼ c. orange zest

1 tsp. vanilla bean powder or vanilla extract

¼ c. agave nectar

FILLING

2¼ c. cashews

1 tsp. vanilla bean powder or vanilla extract

1 c. melted coconut oil (see page 28)

½ c. agave nectar

Juice of ½ lemon

Juice of ½ orange

TOPPING

1 mango, pitted and peeled

2 tbsp. agave nectar

1 tsp. lemon juice

This bright and cheery dessert is guaranteed to bring a smile to your face, if not from its zesty color, then definitely from that first bursting-with-flavor bite. If you're a mango lover like me this may very well become your new favorite treat.

To make the crust: Place the pecans, almonds, Brazil nuts, dried cranberries, orange zest, vanilla bean powder, and agave nectar in a food processor and process until crumbs stick together when pressed between your fingers. Press the crust into the bottom of an 8x8″ square pan. Set aside and make the filling.

To make the filling: Place the cashews in a food processor and process until a fine flour forms. Add the vanilla bean powder, coconut oil, agave nectar, lemon juice, and orange juice and process until smooth and creamy. Pour the filling over the crust. Make the topping.

To make the topping: Place the mango, agave nectar, and lemon juice in a blender and blend until smooth. Pour on top of the cake filling and smooth out with an offset spatula. Place the cake in the freezer until firm enough to cut, 2–4 hours. Cut into a 7x7 grid to make 49 cubes. Serve immediately or store in the refrigerator for up to 3 days.

♥ MAKE IT YOUR OWN ♥

FIG BLISS ENERGY BALLS

Yield: 36 balls
Prep time: 10 minutes

1 c. almonds
²/₃ c. dried figs (approximately 10 dried figs)
1 tsp. vanilla bean powder or vanilla extract
⅛ tsp. sea salt
1 tbsp. coconut nectar

Not counting Fig Newtons, dried figs have long taken a backseat to other dried fruit like raisins and apricots. They're so wonderful, though, that I want to bring them to the forefront. Here they add richness to these energy balls, a great 3 p.m., afternoon-slump-deflecting snack. Enjoy with a cup of fresh dairy-free milk or tea.

Place the almonds, dried figs, vanilla bean powder, sea salt, and coconut nectar in a food processor and process until the dough sticks together when you press it between your fingers.

Using a melon baller, place a scoop of dough into the palm of your hand. Shape into a smooth and round ball, about 1″ in diameter. Set the balls on a tray and repeat to make approximately 36 balls. Serve immediately or store in a cool, dry place for up to 3 days.

························· ♥ TIPS & TRICKS ♥ ·····················

I like to lightly coat my palms with coconut oil before shaping the dough into balls. This ensures that it won't stick, and it gives the balls a pretty sheen. I also coat the melon baller with the coconut oil, which helps the dough slide right out.

♥ MAKE IT YOUR OWN ♥

CHOCO-LATTE COOKIES

Yield: 18 cookies
Prep time: 15 minutes

½ c. almond flour
½ c. coconut flour
⅓ c. cacao powder
⅓ c. coconut crystals
1½ tsp. espresso powder
½ tsp. vanilla bean powder
or vanilla extract
Pinch of sea salt
10 pitted dates
3 tbsp. almond milk
3 tbsp. coconut nectar
2 tbsp. almond butter
1½ tsp. coffee extract
⅓ c. cacao nibs
Coconut palm sugar or raw
cane sugar, for garnish

One of the joys of my childhood was spending the day with my grandfather, who often let us help him recycle soda cans. We'd load up the back of his Chevy pickup with as many bags of cans as we could safely fit, then drive the distance from Revere to the recycling center in Boston. Once we arrived at the recycling center, my sisters and I would step aside while our strong grandpa tossed the big black bags over his shoulder, just like Santa Claus—and with his jolly smile, rosy cheeks, and sacks of treasure, he wasn't far off from the real thing! Then, can by can, we'd carefully unload our bounty onto a conveyer belt. When our work was done we'd be rewarded with coins and treated to a taco lunch at our favorite place to eat—Taco Bell. After lunch he'd let us pick out a sweet; he always chose something chocolate. And so it was that I was thinking about my grandfather when I developed these rich, chocolaty cookies. I think they'd be right up his alley!

Line a platter with parchment paper.

In a large mixing bowl or the bowl of an electric mixer, combine the almond flour, coconut flour, cacao powder, coconut crystals, espresso powder, vanilla bean powder, and sea salt. Gently mix with the whisk attachment of the mixer until well incorporated, approximately 30 seconds.

Add the dates, almond milk, coconut nectar, almond butter, and coffee extract to the bowl and mix again for 30 seconds or until well incorporated. Add the cacao nibs and mix until thoroughly combined.

Using an ice-cream scoop, scoop balls of dough onto the parchment paper. Lightly flatten with the palm of your hand. Turn the cookies over and, using the back of a fork, make impressions in two directions (one horizontal, one vertical—they'll cross in the middle) on top of the cookie. Lightly sprinkle sugar on top for garnish. Store in a cool, dry place for up to 3 days.

♥ TIPS & TRICKS ♥

For a firmer cookie, refrigerate before serving. For a crunchier cookie, dehydrate them in a 108°F oven for 8 hours.

♥ SAVOR THIS ♥

Many people avoid chocolate because they think it's fattening, addictive, and nutritionally void. The truth is, pure cacao from the cacao bean is highly nutritious and has a number of health benefits. Not only is it full of fiber, magnesium, and iron, but it's also rich in anti-oxidants. Pure cacao (cocoa) may also have the ability to boost endorphins, which makes us feel happy in the same way that other endorphin-boosting activities (like exercising or laughing) do. Cacao does contain caffeine, something to consider when deciding whether or not it's for you. But also listen to your body: it will tell you whether cacao is the right choice (and for most of us, it is!).

♥ MAKE IT YOUR OWN ♥

RASPBERRY AND COCONUT GLAZED DOUGHNUTS

Yield: 20 mini doughnuts

Prep time: 30 minutes, plus 30 minutes for doughnuts to set

DOUGHNUT BASE

12 pitted deglet dates

1 c. almond flour

½ c. coconut flour

¼ c. coconut flakes

2 tsp. coconut sugar

1 tsp. vanilla bean powder or vanilla extract

¼ c. agave nectar

PINK GLAZE

⅔ c. raspberries

½ tsp. vanilla bean powder or vanilla extract

⅓ c. coconut butter, softened

¼ c. coconut milk

3 tbsp. agave nectar

1 tbsp. lemon juice

Coconut flakes, for garnish

Doughnuts are the last treat you'd expect to find on a raw food roster, but these do the genre proud. Once you get the base down, you can run with it, creating variations from chocolate doughnuts with sprinkles to maple bars. This recipe calls for a doughnut pan; if you don't have one, simply shape the dough into O's with your hands.

Lightly grease a doughnut pan with coconut oil. Line a tray with parchment paper.

To make the doughnut base: Place the dates, almond flour, coconut flour, coconut flakes, coconut sugar, and vanilla bean powder in a food processor. Process until well combined. While the machine is running, pour the agave nectar in through the top, processing until the dough sticks together, approximately 15 seconds.

Divide the dough into 20 small pieces and firmly press the pieces into the doughnut pan. If you don't have a doughnut pan, shape the doughnuts and place them on the parchment-lined tray. Set in the refrigerator while you make the glaze.

To make the pink glaze: Place the raspberries, vanilla bean powder, coconut butter, coconut milk, agave nectar, and lemon juice in a blender and blend until smooth. Pour into a medium bowl.

To assemble: Remove the doughnuts from the pan by tracing the outside of the doughnuts with an offset spatula, gently lifting around the edges until they pop out. Working one at a time, place each doughnut in the glaze bowl so one side gets coated with glaze, then lift it from the bowl with a fork. Tap the fork against the rim of the bowl to allow excess glaze to drip off and place the doughnut, glaze side up, on the parchment-lined tray. Repeat until all the doughnuts are coated.

Sprinkle coconut flakes onto the wet doughnuts and refrigerate for 30 minutes or until the glaze hardens. Serve immediately or store in the refrigerator for up to 3 days.

♥ MAKE IT YOUR OWN ♥

♥ MAKE IT YOUR OWN ♥

CINNAMON RAISIN SUNFLOWER TWISTS

Yield: 5 twists
Prep time: 15 minutes, plus 15 minutes for glaze to set

One day I set out to make a nut-free raisin cookie, but perfection eluded me. I began to play with the dough to see what else I could come up with when, suddenly, a light bulb went off. When I was growing up, I frequented a doughnut shop by my house that made an incredible cinnamon raisin twist. With a few turns of the wrist, I turned the cookie dough into this trip down memory lane. I like the new version even better.

To make the twist dough: Place the sunflower seeds and flax meal in a food processor and process until a fine flour forms. (Do not overprocess or you'll create a butter.) Add the raisins, vanilla bean powder, and cinnamon and process again. With the machine running, add the maple syrup; stop as soon as the dough forms a ball.

Transfer the dough to a surface lined with parchment paper or a Silpat mat and divide into 5 pieces. Roll each piece into a strand approximately 16" long. Fold each strand into a U shape, then crisscross the two sides to create a twist. When you reach the end, pinch the ends together. Place the twists in the refrigerator and make the glaze.

To make the glaze: Place the coconut oil, maple syrup, and vanilla extract in a small bowl and whisk to combine. Gently brush the glaze onto each twist with a pastry brush or drizzle using a spoon. Transfer to the refrigerator until the glaze hardens, about 15 minutes. Serve immediately or store in the refrigerator for up to 3 days.

TWIST DOUGH

1 c. sunflower seeds

2 tbsp. flax meal

½ c. raisins

½ tsp. vanilla bean powder or vanilla extract

1 tsp. ground cinnamon

3 tbsp. maple syrup

GLAZE

2 tbsp. melted coconut oil (see page 28)

1 tbsp. maple syrup

½ tsp. vanilla extract

BOSTON CREAM CUPS

Yield: 6 large cups
Prep time: 40 minutes, plus 15 minutes for chocolate to set

BASE

1 c. almond flour

½ c. coconut flour

½ c. cashew flour

1 tsp. vanilla bean powder or vanilla extract

¼ c. agave nectar

CREAM

¼ banana (approximately 3″)

¼ c. chilled coconut cream or cashew almond cream (page 28 or 29)

1 tbsp. coconut nectar

½ tsp. butterscotch extract

¼ tsp. maple syrup

¼ tsp. vanilla extract

CHOCOLATE SAUCE

3 tbsp. cacao powder

2 tbsp. lucuma powder

½ c. melted cacao butter (see page 27)

2 tbsp. agave nectar

I have a weakness for anything chocolaty with a custard-like filling. While growing up in Massachusetts I'd be torn between the strawberry and the Boston cream doughnuts at our local sweet shop. Sometimes I'd beg my parents to buy both. Looking back, I think what I loved most about the Boston cream doughnut was the element of surprise. You bite into pastry and suddenly your mouth is filled with luscious cream. These Boston Cream Cups, although much healthier than the doughnuts of my youth, offer the same sort of delicious surprise in the center.

To make the base: Place the almond flour, coconut flour, cashew flour, and vanilla bean powder in a food processor. Process until well combined, then as the processor is running, add the agave nectar. The mixture will remain crumbly looking but will stick together. Stop the processor once the mixture holds together when pressed between your fingers.

Remove one-third of the base mixture from the food processor and form it into a ball. On a piece of parchment paper, flatten the ball to a ¼″ thickness using a rolling pin or the palm of your hand. Cut out 6 circles with a cookie cutter or the mouth of a glass (you may need a paring knife to help if you use a glass). Place the circles on a plate and refrigerate until needed.

Divide the remaining two-thirds of the mixture among 6 cupcake liners, pressing the dough into the bottoms of the liners and up the sides about two-thirds of the way. (It helps to place the liners in a cupcake pan so you can press against it when shaping these cups). Set the pan in the refrigerator while you make the cream.

To make the cream: Place the banana, coconut cream, coconut nectar, butterscotch extract, maple syrup, and vanilla extract in a blender and blend until smooth.

To assemble: Scoop 1 tbsp. of the cream into each cup. Place the circles on top of each cup and gently press the edges together. Set aside and make the chocolate sauce.

To make the chocolate sauce: Whisk together the cacao powder, lucuma powder, cacao butter, and agave nectar in a small bowl. Pour the chocolate on top of the cups and gently swirl it so that it covers the entire top of the cup and evenly drips down the edges. Set the cups in the refrigerator until the chocolate hardens, approximately 10–15 minutes. Serve immediately or store in the refrigerator for up to 2 days.

♥ MAKE IT YOUR OWN ♥

SPICED CARAMEL APPLE MUFFINS

Yield: 6 large muffins
Prep time: 30 minutes

APPLE FILLING

3 Fuji apples, peeled, cored, and cubed

2 tbsp. coconut crystals

1 tbsp. peeled and grated ginger

Juice of 1 lemon

MUFFIN BASE

1½ c. almond flour

¼ c. coconut flour

3 tbsp. coconut crystals

1½ tsp. vanilla bean powder or vanilla extract

1½ tsp. ground cinnamon

¼ tsp. ground cloves

½ c. coconut nectar

2 tbsp. almond butter

CARAMEL SAUCE

¾ c. melted cacao butter (see page 27)

¼ c. lucuma powder

¾ c. coconut nectar

"Plant the seeds and they will grow . . ." I was reminded of this saying as I was traveling through apple and pumpkin orchards in the beautiful rolling hills of Comstock Park, Michigan, one dewy and slightly cool yet humid morning. Our host, Rose, took Alex and I on a seven-mile road trip outside of downtown Grand Rapids to an orchard that she favored as a young girl. The orchard grew a large variety, ranging from Fuji (my all-time favorite) to the delicious Honeycrisp. It was a dream come true: I had fantasized about apple picking when I was a kid. At the time, I was also entertaining another dream come true by growing our own little "apple"—that is, our son—so things just couldn't get any better. I had been craving apples all throughout my pregnancy, so it wasn't by happenstance that I was referring to the baby as our little "apple." Maybe we really are what we eat.

If you find apples as inspiring as I do, these muffins were made for you. They get a kick from fresh ginger and a spicy sweetness from apple's natural partners, cinnamon and cloves. The finishing touch is a drizzle of caramel, which, after it firms up in the refrigerator, gives the muffins a bit of crackle as you bite into them.

Line a muffin tin with 6 liners.

To make the apple filling: Place the apples in a medium bowl. Add the coconut crystals, ginger, and lemon juice and mix with a spoon until the apples are well coated. Set half of the apple mixture aside (you'll use this as a topping later) and transfer the other half to a blender. Blend into a lightly chunky applesauce. Set aside and make the muffin base.

To make the muffin base: Place the almond flour, coconut flour, coconut crystals, vanilla bean powder, cinnamon, and cloves in a food processor. Process until well combined. With the machine running, add the coconut nectar and almond butter. Process until the mixture just sticks together. Be careful not to overprocess.

To assemble: Press half the muffin base into the cupcake liners, leaving a deep well in the center for the apple filling. Fill the well to the top with the applesauce.

Turn the remaining half of the muffin base out onto a flat surface lined with parchment paper and shape into a flat rectangle. Using a circle cookie cutter, a glass, or a knife, cut out thin circles and place them over the apple filling to enclose the muffin. Press gently around the edges to seal the muffin top to the base.

Spoon the reserved apple mixture onto the muffin tops, approximately 1 tbsp. per muffin. Set aside and make the caramel sauce.

To make the caramel sauce: Place the melted cacao butter in a small bowl. Whisk in the lucuma powder and coconut nectar until smooth. Drizzle the caramel sauce over the muffins until well coated. Serve immediately while deliciously gooey or store in the refrigerator for up to 3 days.

♥ MAKE IT YOUR OWN ♥

FOUR

PUDDINGS AND PARFAITS

MAPLE BUTTERSCOTCH PUDDING

Yield: 4 servings

Prep time: 10 minutes, plus about 2 hours for pudding to set

If you're like me, you probably grew up knowing pudding as something that came from a package or maybe in a little snack-pack cup. Those convenience puddings had their pleasures but hardly compare to pudding made from scratch. One of my favorite flavors of pudding during my childhood was butterscotch. I've given it a reboot, using coconut cream and cashew almond cream to lend body (it's so much healthier than the usual cream) and infuse the pudding with a bit of tropical flavor.

3 c. coconut meat (about 3 coconuts)

1 large banana, peeled and frozen

1 c. cashew almond cream (page 29)

¼ c. coconut nectar

2 tsp. butterscotch extract

1 tsp. vanilla extract

1 tsp. maple extract or maple syrup

Coconut cream, maple syrup, and coconut crystals, for garnish (optional)

Place the coconut meat, banana, cashew almond cream, coconut nectar, butterscotch extract, vanilla extract, and maple extract in a food processor or blender and process until smooth. Divide among four 4-oz. ramekins and place in the refrigerator until firm, approximately 2 hours.

If desired, garnish each ramekin with a dollop of coconut cream, a drizzle of maple syrup, and a light sprinkle of coconut crystals before serving. Serve immediately or store in the refrigerator for up to 3 days.

♥ SAVOR THIS ♥

Butterscotch is generally made with a lot of brown sugar and butter (though not Scotch, as is sometimes thought). In other words, it's not exactly a health food. Although delicious, it lacks inner beauty. My simple replacement for it is a mix of butterscotch extract (a lot of flavor without all the saturated fat and sugar), maple syrup, and coconut. I think it captures the creamy butterscotch-y flavor we all love so much without the sugar rush. You can take this same mix and add it to cakes or spoon it over ice cream.

POTS DE CRÈME AU CHOCOLAT

Yield: 4 servings

Prep time: 10 minutes, plus 2–3 hours for cream to set

½ oz. Irish moss, soaked and drained (see page 28), or 2 tbsp. melted coconut butter

¾ c. chilled coconut cream

½ c. cacao powder, plus more for garnish

¼ c. coconut nectar

Seeds from a 2″ piece of vanilla bean

Cacao nibs, for garnish (optional)

Chocolate cream made the traditional way is tricky and time-consuming. So you're not going to believe how easy this version is—and yet it's as rich and chocolaty as can be. If you like, serve with a dollop of coconut cream on top.

Place the Irish moss and coconut cream in a blender and blend until smooth. Add the cacao powder, coconut nectar, and vanilla bean seeds and blend briefly until combined. Divide the mixture among four 4-oz. ramekins and refrigerate until firm, approximately 2–3 hours. Serve immediately or store in the refrigerator for up to 3 days. If desired, garnish with cacao nibs and a dusting of cacao powder.

♥ MAKE IT YOUR OWN ♥

RED VELVET CHIA PARFAIT

Yield: 4 parfaits
Prep time: 15 minutes

Parfaits provide a lot of payoff for very little effort—in 15 minutes you can have a beautiful, deliciously creamy dessert. This parfait is notable for the raw vegan cream cheese frosting on top. It's wonderful spread on cakes and cupcakes, too. If you like a sweeter frosting, feel free to add 2 tbsp. of your favorite sweetener.

To make the parfait base: Combine the chia seeds, cacao powder, almond milk, beet juice, coconut nectar, and vanilla bean powder in a medium bowl and whisk until well incorporated. Let the mixture sit for 10 minutes to thicken. Make the frosting.

To make the frosting: Place the melted coconut oil, coconut cream, lemon juice, and vanilla extract in the bowl of an electric mixer or a large bowl. Beat on medium speed or whisk by hand until the mixture is whipped and well incorporated. Don't overmix or the frosting will be runny.

To assemble: Divide the chia mixture among 4 parfait glasses or bowls.

Place a frosting bag (or plastic bag) inside a glass, allowing the top of the bag to fold over the outside of the glass. This will allow you to scoop frosting into the bag without the risk of it leaking. Fill the bag with the frosting, then squeeze a dollop into each parfait glass on top of the chia mixture. Add the garnish and serve immediately, or store in the refrigerator for up to 3 days.

PARFAIT BASE

¼ c. chia seeds (black or white or a mix of the two)

1 tbsp. cacao powder

2 c. almond milk

2 tsp. beet juice or natural red food coloring

1½ tsp. coconut nectar

¼ tsp. vanilla bean powder or vanilla extract

"CREAM CHEESE" FROSTING

4 tbsp. melted coconut oil (see page 28)

2 c. chilled coconut cream

1 tbsp. Meyer lemon juice (regular lemon juice works, too)

1 tsp. vanilla extract

Chocolate curls or cacao powder, for garnish

♥ MAKE IT YOUR OWN ♥

_____

_____

_____

_____

CLEMENTINE COULIS

Yield: 4 servings

Prep time: 30 minutes, plus 3 hours for cream to set

CREAM

2 c. coconut cream

2 tbsp. melted coconut oil (see page 28)

1 tbsp. coconut nectar

Seeds from a 4" piece of vanilla bean

FRUIT TOPPING

6 clementines, peeled and, if necessary, seeded

¼ tsp. vanilla bean powder or vanilla extract

1 tbsp. coconut nectar

1 clementine, peeled and separated into sections, for garnish

¼ c. pomegranate seeds, for garnish

To make this wintertime treat, you mold the cream, then top it with a clementine sauce—and the contrast of the bright orange coulis against the white cream is absolutely beautiful! You can use any kind of tangerine in this recipe (and even oranges in a pinch), but try to find seedless varieties. That will make preparing the coulis a little easier.

To make the cream: Place the coconut cream, coconut oil, coconut nectar, and vanilla bean seeds in the bowl of an electric mixer or, if you're using a handheld mixer, a large bowl. Whip for 1 minute, then divide the cream among four 4-oz. ramekins. Place the ramekins in the refrigerator for 3 hours to allow the cream to set, and begin making the fruit topping.

To make the fruit topping: Place the clementines, vanilla bean powder, and coconut nectar in a food processor and process until smooth. Strain through a fine-mesh sieve, collecting the juice in a separate bowl. Place the fruit puree in the refrigerator and, if desired, save the juice for another use.

To assemble: Remove the coconut cream from the refrigerator. Using a spatula, gently loosen the cream in the ramekins. Place a small plate over one ramekin and invert it to transfer the cream to the plate. Repeat with the other ramekins. Carefully arrange the molded cream on a large plate.

Pour the fruit topping over the cream. Scatter the clementine slices and pomegranate seeds around the cream to garnish. Serve immediately or store in the refrigerator for up to 2 days.

MACA-CHIA PROTEIN PUDDING

Yield: 2 servings

Prep time: 5 minutes, plus 1–2 hours for pudding to set

½ **medium banana**

2–3 pitted dates

2½ tbsp. white or black chia seeds

2 tbsp. cacao powder

1 tsp. maca

1 c. almond milk

2 tbsp. almond butter

Chopped nuts, for garnish (optional)

Cacao nibs, for garnish (optional)

Feeling lethargic? This pudding will energize you. Not only does it contain chia seeds, famously used for stamina by the best runners in the world—the Tarahumara Indians, who run for hundreds of miles at a time—but it also provides a dollop of maca, an Andean herb also thought to help stave off fatigue. Chia is also packed with protein—nearly 5 grams per ounce.

Place the banana, dates, chia seeds, cacao powder, maca, almond milk, and almond butter in a blender and blend until smooth. Pour into 2 small bowls or ramekins, cover, and place in the refrigerator. Chill until the ingredients gel, about 1–2 hours. If desired, garnish with chopped nuts and cacao nibs. Serve immediately or store in the refrigerator for up to 3 days.

♥ MAKE IT YOUR OWN ♥

JASON MRAZ'S CHOCOMOLE

Yield: 4 servings
Prep time: 5 minutes

I've been a fan of Jason Mraz for years. His songs are so uplifting. They express happiness, health, creativity, and playfulness—all the good things in life. There isn't much on par with Jason's music, but his chocolate pudding—he's dubbed it chocomole—comes pretty close. It's delicious! I am so honored to have him contribute his recipe to Love Fed. *Enjoy this decadent pudding while dancing around to "I'm Yours" in your kitchen—that's what I'll be doing!*

4 ripe avocados
2 c. cacao powder
16 pitted medjool dates
1 tsp. vanilla extract
¼ c. agave nectar
2 heaping tsp. coconut oil
Pinch sea salt, for garnish

Cut avocados in half and remove the skin and pits. Place the avocado halves, cacao powder, dates, vanilla extract, agave nectar, and coconut oil in a blender and blend until smooth. Garnish with sea salt and serve.

♥ MAKE IT YOUR OWN ♥

_____
_____
_____
_____

MAPLE BANANA TIRAMISU TRIFLE

Yield: 2 mini trifles
Prep time: 30 minutes

CREAM

1 c. cashews, soaked and drained (see page 29)

⅛ tsp. sea salt

¼ c. almond milk

¼ c. cold-brewed coffee (see page 42) or 1 tsp. coffee extract

¼ c. maple syrup

1 tbsp. melted coconut oil (see page 28)

1 tsp. vanilla extract

1 tsp. lemon juice

CHOCOLATE SAUCE DRIZZLE

1 tbsp. cacao powder

1 tbsp. maple syrup

¼ tsp. vanilla extract

3 bananas

1½ tsp. cacao powder, for garnish

This is my raw-vegan mash-up of two favorite European desserts: English trifle and Italian tiramisu. The result is a sophisticated dessert worthy of any fancy tabletop.

To make the cream: Place the cashews, sea salt, almond milk, cold-brewed coffee, maple syrup, coconut oil, vanilla extract, and lemon juice in a blender and blend until very creamy.

To make the chocolate sauce drizzle: Whisk the cacao powder, maple syrup, and vanilla extract together in a small bowl until smooth. Transfer to a squirt bottle, if you have one, or leave in the bowl until ready to use.

To assemble the trifle: Cut each of the bananas into 3 even sections. Slice each section in half lengthwise (you will have 18 total pieces of banana). Place 2 of the banana sections in the bottom of a 3¾x4¼″ trifle glass or ramekin. Repeat in a second glass or ramekin. Squirt chocolate sauce (or drizzle with a spoon) along the rims of the glasses all the way around, reserving some for garnish. Next, add enough cream to cover the bananas. Layer another 2 banana sections on top, then the cream.

Stand up the remaining 10 banana sections vertically around the sides of each glass (5 per glass), then pour in the cream to the top. Gently sift cacao powder on top and garnish with a drizzle of chocolate sauce. Serve immediately or let chill in the refrigerator for 30 minutes or until ready to serve. The trifles can be stored in the refrigerator for up to 3 days.

♥ MAKE IT YOUR OWN ♥

FIVE

ICE CREAM, YOGURT, AND FROZEN TREATS

PISTACHIO SAFFRON ROSE WATER ICE CREAM

Yield: 6 servings

Prep time: 55 minutes, plus about 2 hours refrigerating and freezing time

2 tsp. saffron threads

3 tbsp. warm filtered water

½ c. coconut crystals

¼ c. pistachios, plus more for garnish

1 oz. Irish moss, soaked and drained (see page 28)

2 c. regular coconut milk

1 c. light coconut milk

¼ c. coconut nectar

5 tbsp. rose water

Ice-cream parlors have never been more inventive than now, offering flavors way beyond the once-exotic cookies 'n cream. Now you too can make a complex-tasting ice cream at home, and without a drop of cow's milk. Saffron and rose water coconut has to be my favorite ice-cream flavor of all time. It's rich and creamy but still light and refreshing.

Crush the saffron between your fingers and soak in the warm filtered water for 20 minutes.

Place the saffron, saffron soaking water, coconut crystals, pistachios, Irish moss, coconut milk, light coconut milk, coconut nectar, and rose water in a blender. Blend on high speed until well mixed. Place the blender jar in the refrigerator to chill for at least 1 hour.

Transfer the mixture to an ice-cream maker and churn until thick and scoopable, approximately 30 minutes or less depending on your machine. (Alternatively, pour the ice-cream mixture into a freezable container and once it's firmed up to your liking, dig in.)

Transfer to the freezer to harden more, about 30 minutes. When ready to serve, garnish with chopped pistachios. Store any remaining ice cream in the freezer.

♥ TIPS & TRICKS ♥

If you have trouble locating Irish moss, you can leave it out; your ice cream will still be creamy if not quite as thick. A professional chef—or professional ice-cream eater—may be the only one who can tell a difference.

♥ **SAVOR THIS** ♥

Saffron has been an extremely precious spice for thousands of years owing to its rich color, flavor, and scent, and the time it takes to harvest. Saffron's legacy remains today. A little bit can go a long way—just a couple of threads lend enough spice to color and flavor an entire meal. Saffron can be costly because the saffron stigmas, the part commonly used for cooking, must be removed from the crocus flower by hand—and it takes 4,500 crocus flowers to produce 1 oz. of saffron. Think about it: a lot of love goes into that work.

Saffron is a good source of minerals like copper, potassium, calcium, manganese, iron, selenium, zinc, and magnesium. It is also rich in many vitamins, including vitamin A, folic acid, riboflavin, niacin, and vitamin C.

♥ MAKE IT YOUR OWN ♥

BE MY BUTTERCUP ICE CREAM

Yield: 6 servings

Prep time: 45 minutes, plus about 3 hours refrigerating and freezing time

1 c. almond butter

⅔ c. coconut crystals

1 c. coconut milk

2 c. cashew almond cream (page 29)

1 tsp. coffee extract

1 tsp. vanilla extract

12 Crunchy Peanut Butter Cup candies made with almond butter, chopped (page 168)

I made this recipe for my sweetheart on Valentine's Day due to what you might call divine dessert intervention. I didn't plan anything extra special or out of the ordinary for the day—no special meal, no chocolate, no flowers. But when I was cleaning out my refrigerator I stumbled upon coconut milk and cashew almond cream that was about to expire and needed to be used. I also had a batch of Crunchy Peanut Butter Cups that I'd made earlier hanging around. Could they all work together? Turns out they could. You never know when a little of this and a little of that is going to turn into a favorite recipe. Be My Buttercup Ice Cream is now a regular part of my repertoire.

Add the almond butter and coconut crystals to the bowl of an electric mixer or, if using a hand mixer, a medium bowl. Beat on low speed until smooth. Add the coconut milk and mix on low until the coconut crystals are dissolved. Stir in the cashew almond cream, coffee extract, and vanilla extract. Cover and refrigerate for anywhere from 2 hours to overnight.

Transfer the mixture to an ice-cream maker and churn. After 15 minutes, add the peanut butter cup candies, then continue churning until soft and creamy, but scoopable, about 15 more minutes, depending on your machine. (Alternatively, pour the ice-cream mixture into a freezable container and once it's firmed up to your liking, dig in.) Transfer to the freezer to harden more, about 30 minutes, then serve. Store any remaining ice cream in the freezer.

> ················· ♥ TIPS & TRICKS ♥ ·················
>
> Don't have a mixer? Don't worry! You can make this recipe using your blender. Simply add all the ingredients except for the peanut butter cups and blend until well mixed, then proceed as you would if you'd used a mixer.

CHOCOLATE CORIANDER ICE CREAM

Yield: 2 servings

Prep time: 45 minutes, plus about 1 hour and 45 minutes refrigerating and freezing time

½ c. cacao powder

2 tsp. ground coriander

½ tsp. vanilla bean powder or vanilla extract

Very fine zest of 1 unripened orange (use ripe if you can't find unripe)

¾ c. coconut cream

¼ c. coconut nectar

2 tsp. orange blossom water

2 tbsp. cacao nibs

Fresh cilantro, for garnish (optional)

Orange zest, for garnish (optional)

One lovely afternoon I stumbled upon a tree that had a lot of green citrus fruits on it. Naturally, I thought the little green fruits were limes, so I picked a few only to discover that they were unripened oranges. Now that I'd picked them I had two options: toss them back to nature or transform them into a dish. Stumped at how I might be able to use unripened oranges, I still chose to take them home. They sat on my counter for a few days until a light bulb went off. The result was this chocolate coriander ice cream with a hint of unripened orange zest. Those young oranges taught me a lot about inspiration and reminded me to be patient and not give up on anything too soon. If you wait for ideas, they inevitably come.

Place the cacao powder, coriander, vanilla bean powder, orange zest, coconut cream, coconut nectar, and orange blossom water in a blender and blend until smooth and creamy. Transfer the blender container to the refrigerator and chill the mixture for a minimum of 1 hour.

Pour the chilled mixture into an ice-cream maker and follow the manufacturer's instructions, churning for approximately 30 minutes, depending on your machine. (Alternatively, pour the ice-cream mixture into a freezable container and once it's firmed up to your liking, dig in.) Fold the cacao nibs into the ice cream during the last minute of mixing.

Transfer to the freezer to harden more, about 30 minutes, then serve. If desired, garnish with fresh cilantro and orange zest. Store any remaining ice cream in the freezer.

♥ MAKE IT YOUR OWN ♥

NUT-ELLA GELATO

Yield: 4 servings
Prep time: 30 minutes, plus 2 hours and 30 minutes refrigerating time

ICE-CREAM BASE

⅔ c. coconut crystals

⅛ tsp. fine sea salt

2 c. cashew cream (page 29)

1 tsp. vanilla extract

¼ tsp. guar gum

FOR THE NUT-ELLA

2 c. hazelnuts

1 c. coconut crystals

¼ c. cacao powder

¼ tsp. fine sea salt

3 tbsp. melted coconut oil or cacao butter (see page 28 or 27)

1 tsp. vanilla bean powder or vanilla extract

We all know that one person who commands attention when walking into a room and who exudes humor and nuttiness along with poise and charm. Well, that's my friend Ella. Like Ella, this recipe is full of beauty and nuttiness! It's my homage to her. As you're making it, you may be surprised at how long it takes to turn the nuts into nut butter. But don't worry; they will get there. First you'll see the nuts turning into coarse chunks. Soon after you will see a meal or flour form. Then, finally, the nuts will turn smooth and creamy.

To make the base: In a medium bowl, blend the coconut crystals, sea salt, cashew cream, vanilla extract, and guar gum until they form a light brown nut milk. Place in the refrigerator until well chilled, approximately 2 hours. While the base is chilling, make the nut-ella.

To make the nut-ella: Place the hazelnuts in a food processor and process, scraping down the sides occasionally, until a smooth, creamy butter forms. (It may take as long as 15 minutes.)

Using a coffee or spice grinder, grind the coconut crystals into a very fine powder. (This step is optional.)

Add the coconut crystals, cacao powder, and sea salt to the nut butter. Slowly add the coconut oil as the processor is running. Once completely combined and liquefied, stir in the vanilla bean powder, pour the nut butter mixture into a glass measuring cup, and let cool to room temperature.

To make the ice cream: Once the ice-cream base mixture has chilled, pour it into an ice-cream maker and let it churn until it begins to thicken evenly, about 15 minutes. Add the nut-ella and continue churning until the ice cream is thick, creamy, and scoopable, about 15 minutes more, depending on your machine. (Alternatively, combine the ice-cream base and nut-ella and pour into a freezable container.) Once it's firmed up to your liking, serve immediately or store in the freezer.

BLUEBERRY COCONUT DREAMSICLES

Yield: 5 dreamsicles
Prep time: 5 minutes, plus 2–6 hours freezing time

When my local Whole Foods Market sponsored a Blueberry Blast-Off Blog Challenge, I was excited—I have a ferocious appetite for all things blueberry. The contest specified using only ten ingredients, a breeze for me, since I tend to keep things simple anyway. The hard part was deciding which blueberry recipe to go with. In the end, nothing called to me more than the humble elegance of homemade Blueberry Coconut Dreamsicles.

A dreamsicle is my version of the creamsicle, which, if you grew up in the 1980s like I did, will probably be familiar. They're usually orange flavored, a pairing of sweet cream and citrus nectar. I thought the idea would translate well to blueberry and coconut cream (and be even more delectable, hence the name dreamsicle), and it did. I can guarantee kids of all ages (aka everyone) will appreciate these blueberries and cream pops.

If you like, replace your pop mold's sticks with 6" twigs for a rustic look.

1 c. blueberries

2 tbsp. coconut nectar or sweetener of your choice (optional)

Juice of 1 lemon

1½ c. coconut cream

In a medium bowl, combine the blueberries, coconut nectar (if desired), and lemon juice. Mix lightly to coat the berries.

Place the coconut cream in a second medium bowl. Adding the blueberry mixture a few spoonfuls at a time, whip with a handheld electric mixer or whisk until thickened. Some of the berries will break down, releasing their juices and creating texture. If you want the berries whole, gently hand mix them into the cream using a rubber spatula. If you prefer a quicker method and a more vibrant purple pop, simply blend all the ingredients together in a blender.

Pour the mixture into pop molds. Freeze for 2–6 hours or until completely firm. Run the mold under warm water for a few seconds and gently remove the pops. Serve immediately or store in the freezer.

BANANA MAPLE PECAN SPLIT

Yield: 4 servings
Prep time: 20 minutes, plus 2–4 hours freezing time

ICE-CREAM BASE

4 ripe bananas, peeled and frozen

1 tsp. vanilla bean powder or vanilla extract

½ tsp. ground cinnamon

¼ c. maple syrup

MIX-INS

¼ c. pecan pieces

1 tbsp. coconut crystals

2 tbsp. maple syrup

MAPLE GLAZE

¼ tsp. ground cinnamon

¼ tsp. vanilla bean powder or vanilla extract

2 tbsp. maple syrup

1 tsp. butterscotch extract

1 banana

Although I still love a simple ice cream, made with pure flavors and little else, I've noticed that the mix-in and topping craze is ever increasing. This recipe will satisfy any mix-ins/toppings fan, while still keeping the dish healthy and exquisitely flavored. You'll notice that the base is built primarily on bananas—no nut or coconut milk required.

To make the ice-cream base: Place the bananas, vanilla bean powder, cinnamon, and maple syrup in a food processor and process until well incorporated. Pour the mixture into a freezer-safe container and freeze for 2–4 hours, or until frozen. Assemble the mix-ins.

To assemble the mix-ins: In a small bowl, combine the pecan pieces, coconut crystals, and maple syrup and stir until well coated. Make the glaze.

To make the glaze: In a small bowl, whisk together the cinnamon, vanilla bean powder, maple syrup, and butterscotch extract until well combined.

To assemble: Just before serving, scoop ice cream into bowls, slice the banana into quarters and place around the ice cream, garnish with the mix-ins, then drizzle the glaze over the top. Store any remaining ice cream in the freezer.

························ ♥ MAKE IT YOUR OWN ♥ ························

PEACHES AND CREAM ICE-CREAM TERRINE

Yield: 8 servings

Prep time: 45 minutes, plus 2–6 hours freezing time

6 peaches, preferably a mix of yellow and white

1½ c. chilled coconut cream

1 tsp. vanilla bean powder or vanilla extract

1 tbsp. honey

Here's some good news: you don't have to peel the peaches to make this terrine. All you have to do is rinse the fruit, then cut them into cubes. That not only makes the prep go more quickly, but the skin also helps give the ice cream a pretty, freckled appearance.

Place a 9x4" loaf pan in the freezer to chill.

Chop the peaches into ¼" cubes. Place half of the cubes in an airtight container and store in the refrigerator. Place the other half in a blender with the coconut cream, vanilla bean powder, and honey. Blend until smooth.

Transfer the blended mixture to an ice-cream maker and process according to the manufacturer's instructions, churning for approximately 30 minutes, depending on your machine. (Alternatively, pour the ice-cream mixture into a freezable container and freeze until firm, 2–4 hours.) Once the ice cream has reached a thick and creamy consistency, add half of the reserved chopped peaches and then churn the mixture for a few minutes more, or until the chopped peaches are well incorporated. (If using a freezable container instead, simply place it back in the freezer while you prepare the loaf pan.)

Meanwhile, line the loaf pan with parchment paper or, for a smoother finish, plastic wrap. Make sure some of the paper or wrap reaches 1–2" past the pan's edges. Spread the ice-cream mixture evenly into the loaf pan using an offset spatula or the back of a large spoon. Cover the ice-cream mixture with parchment paper or plastic wrap and place in the freezer until firm, about 2–6 hours.

Once fully frozen, tug on the paper or wrap to lift the terrine from the pan. Place on a serving dish. Add the remaining chopped peaches to the top of the terrine. Serve immediately or store in the freezer.

♥ MAKE IT YOUR OWN ♥

BEST BASIC VANILLA ICE CREAM

Yield: 4 servings

Prep time: 45 minutes, plus 1 hour refrigerating time

Having a tub of vanilla ice cream in the freezer is like having apples and oranges in the fridge—it's a staple that you'll definitely use whether just as a snack or as the pièce de résistance on top of another dessert. Plus, make and store a batch of this basic vanilla and you'll never be caught short when guests drop in. Top with a scattering of cacao nibs or lavender flowers and you've got a beautiful last-minute treat.

3½ c. coconut meat (about 3–4 coconuts)

1 c. cashews

2 tsp. vanilla bean powder or vanilla extract

1½ c. almond milk

1¼ c. maple syrup

2 tbsp. plus 1 tsp. vanilla extract

Place the coconut meat, cashews, vanilla bean powder, almond milk, maple syrup, and vanilla extract in a blender. Blend on high speed until smooth. Transfer the blender container to the refrigerator and chill the mixture for about 1 hour, or until well chilled.

Pour the chilled mixture into an ice-cream maker and follow the manufacturer's instructions, churning for approximately 30 minutes, depending on your machine. (Alternatively, pour the ice-cream mixture into a freezable container and freeze until firm, 2–4 hours.) Serve immediately or store in the freezer.

♥ MAKE IT YOUR OWN ♥

SUMMER BERRY ICE CREAM

Yield: 2 servings
Prep time: 5 minutes

1 large banana, peeled and frozen

10 frozen strawberries

¾ c. chilled coconut cream

1 tsp. vanilla extract

Fresh berries, for garnish (optional)

Fresh mint leaves, for garnish (optional)

Believe it or not, you don't need to add a drop of sweetener to this summer treat—it gets its sweetness from fruit, and the bananas in particular. I always buy a bunch of bananas especially for freezing. I let them get overripe (this heightens their sweetness, which makes them an especially good ice-cream ingredient), then peel them and place them in a sealed plastic bag so I always have them on hand for spur-of-the-moment treats.

Place the banana, strawberries, coconut cream, and vanilla extract in a blender and blend for about 20 seconds (if using a high-speed blender) or until the frozen fruit is broken down and thoroughly combined with the cream. Do not overblend or it won't be scoopable.* Top with the fresh berries and mint if desired, or simply enjoy as is.

* If you do happen to overblend (don't worry—it happens to the best of us!), simply place the ice cream in a freezable, airtight container and set it in the back of your freezer. Allow it to thicken back up before serving.

♥ MAKE IT YOUR OWN ♥

CHOCOLATE-COVERED ICE-CREAM POPS

Yield: 24 pops
Prep time: 25 minutes

These small pops allow you to indulge without going overboard. You can use any flavor ice cream, but I tend to stick with a classic vanilla and embellish the coating with flavor enhancers like nuts and cacao nibs.

Line a tray with parchment paper.

To make the chocolate shell: Whisk together the cacao powder, cacao butter, and agave nectar in a small bowl and set in a warm spot on your counter.

To assemble the pops: Using a melon baller, scoop a small ball of ice cream. Place a Popsicle stick in the center of the ice-cream ball and quickly dip the ice cream in the chocolate, lifting and turning the stick until all excess chocolate shakes off. You'll want to move quickly—the cold temperature of the ice cream makes the chocolate harden fast. If you're adding garnishes, dip the coated ice cream into a topping immediately after dipping the ice cream in chocolate. Place on the parchment-lined tray and set in the freezer for 10–20 minutes to firm up. Serve immediately or store in the freezer.

CHOCOLATE SHELL
2½ c. cacao powder
2½ c. melted cacao butter (see page 27)
¾ c. agave nectar

1 recipe Best Basic Vanilla Ice Cream (page 141)

OPTIONAL GARNISHES
Chia seeds
Cacao nibs
Goji berries
Cacao powder
Chopped nuts

♥ MAKE IT YOUR OWN ♥

AVOCADO ICE CREAM MINT CHIP SANDWICH

Yield: 4 sandwiches

Prep time: 45 minutes, plus 1 hour refrigerating time

ICE CREAM

1 medium ripe Hass avocado

1 c. chilled coconut cream

1 c. almond milk

¼ c. coconut nectar

1 tsp. vanilla extract

COOKIE DOUGH

1½ c. almond flour

¾ c. cacao powder

¼ c. cacao nibs

¼ tsp. sea salt

1½ tsp. mint extract

½ tsp. vanilla extract

¼ c. coconut nectar

½ c. cacao nibs or hemp seeds, for garnish

Surprised to see avocado in ice cream? Don't let it throw you off: even though avocado is mostly used in savory foods, its mild flavor actually makes it a wonderful addition to sweets, lending both creaminess and healthy fats. Avocado is a great addition to puddings, too. I recommend using Hass avocados—they're unbelievably rich and delicious—but other small California avocados with dense flesh (like Bacon and Fuerte) work well, too.

To make the ice cream: Place the avocado, coconut cream, almond milk, coconut nectar, and vanilla extract in a blender and blend until smooth. Transfer the blender container to the refrigerator and chill the mixture for about 1 hour, or until well chilled. Pour the chilled mixture into an ice-cream maker and follow the manufacturer's instructions, churning for approximately 30 minutes, depending on your machine. (Alternatively, pour the ice-cream mixture into a freezable container and freeze until firm, 2–4 hours.) In the meantime, make the cookie dough.

♥ SAVOR THIS ♥

The Beauty of Avocado

Did you know that the method you use to peel an avocado can change its nutritional value? The part of the avocado with the most nutrients is the dark green layer right underneath the skin. To preserve it, the California Avocado Commission came up with a technique called the "nick and peel" method. First, cut into the avocado lengthwise so that you have two long avocado halves that are still connected in the middle by the seed. Next, twist the halves in opposite directions until they naturally separate. Then remove the seed (I like to hack into the seed with a knife, which then allows you to pull the seed out on the blade without messing up the avocado flesh) and cut each of the halves lengthwise to produce long, quartered sections of the avocado. Use your thumb and index finger to grip the edge of the skin on each quarter and peel it off, just like a banana skin. You'll end up with nice slices that have the green part and its carotenoid antioxidants intact.

Avocado, besides being absolutely delicious, also makes an excellent home remedy hair mask, giving new life to dry, dull, or frizzy locks (the light, moist oils and proteins in avocado help weigh down unruly hair without being too heavy). Here's my recipe for success: mash half of an avocado with 1 tbsp. coconut oil, then massage into clean, damp hair. Let the mask sit for 15 minutes before rinsing with water. Use as frequently as every 2 weeks.

To make the cookie dough: Place the almond flour, cacao powder, cacao nibs, sea salt, mint extract, and vanilla extract in a food processor. Process until well combined. While the lid is still on and the machine is running, add the coconut nectar through the feed tube. Process until the mixture sticks together. Do not overprocess or the dough will be too gooey.

Line your countertop with parchment paper and turn out the dough mixture onto the paper. Form the dough into a rough ball and place another sheet of parchment paper on top. Flatten the dough using the palm of your hand or a rolling pin. Once the dough is flattened, roll it out using a can or rolling pin to ¼″ thickness. Using a round cookie cutter, or by tracing the outline of a cup with a thin, sharp knife, cut 8 circles out of the dough. Set each circle on a plate, layering them one on top of the other, separated by a square of parchment paper to prevent sticking. Set the tray of cookies in the freezer until the sandwiches are ready for assembling.

To assemble the ice-cream sandwiches: Once the ice cream is frozen, place one scoop on top of one cookie circle, and using the back of a spoon or an offset spatula, flatten the ice cream to about 1″ thick. Top with a second cookie. Repeat until all the sandwiches are assembled. Roll the sandwich edges in cacao nibs or hemp seeds for garnish. Serve immediately or store in the freezer.

♥ MAKE IT YOUR OWN ♥

FROZEN COCONUT KEY LIME "CHEESE" CAKE BARS

Yield: 6 bars
Prep time: 20 minutes, plus 4–6 hours freezing time

CHEESECAKE CRUMBLE

¼ c. cashews
1 tbsp. coconut flakes
1 tbsp. coconut nectar
¼ tsp. vanilla extract
¼ tsp. Key lime juice

COCONUT FILLING

2 c. coconut cream
3 tbsp. coconut nectar
1 tsp. vanilla extract
Zest of 1 small Key lime

KEY LIME GELATIN

1 tbsp. agar agar
¼ c. boiling water
¼ tsp. matcha powder
¼ c. melted coconut oil
(see page 28)
2 tbsp. Key lime juice
1 tbsp. honey

I spent many of my formative years in Florida, where Key limes are abundant. They are smaller and sweeter than the common limes sold in most markets. If you can't find them (but try to— they're very special!), a regular lime will do. This recipe also calls for agar agar, a natural gelatin derived from algae. It can usually be purchased where baking and cooking supplies are sold and, of course, can always be found online.

Line a 6x6" square pan with parchment paper.

To make the crumble: Place the cashews, coconut flakes, coconut nectar, vanilla extract, and Key lime juice in a food processor and process until the mixture sticks together. Set aside and make the filling.

To make the coconut filling: Whisk the coconut cream, coconut nectar, vanilla extract, and Key lime zest together in a medium bowl. Pour into the parchment-lined pan and spread evenly with an offset spatula. Make the Key lime gelatin.

To make the Key lime gelatin: In a small bowl, combine the agar agar with the boiling water. Stir until dissolved. Add the matcha powder, coconut oil, Key lime juice, and honey, stirring until well combined. Allow to thicken for a few minutes before assembling the cheesecake.

To assemble the cheesecake: Sprinkle the crumble pieces and gelatin mixture on top of the coconut filling in the pan. Some gelatin will remain on the surface while other parts will sink, creating a beautiful bar once cut. Place the pan in the freezer until the dessert is fully frozen, about 4–6 hours. Cut into six 6x1" bars and serve immediately or store in the freezer.

COCONUT YOGURT

Yield: 2 servings
Prep time: 15 minutes

One of the foods vegans find it hardest to give up is yogurt. Turns out, you don't have to! This yogurt, made from the meat of coconuts, is just as versatile as yogurt made from cow's milk. Top it with fresh or dried fruit, nuts, seeds, spices, and/or sweetener. This yogurt doesn't require fermentation time, so in order to get the benefits of probiotics you can simply mix in a probiotic packet found at most health food stores. Serve as a dessert or even for breakfast with fresh fruit and buckwheat groats drizzled lightly with coconut nectar.

1¼ c. coconut meat (about 3 young or 2 large coconuts)

1 tsp. probiotic/prebiotic powder (optional)

½ tsp. vanilla bean powder or vanilla extract

¼ c. plus 1 tbsp. coconut water

2 tbsp. almond milk

1 tbsp. coconut nectar

1 tsp. lemon juice

Place the coconut meat, probiotic powder (if desired), vanilla bean powder, coconut water, almond milk, coconut nectar, and lemon juice in a food processor or blender and process until creamy. Serve immediately. Store leftover yogurt in the refrigerator for up to 3 days.

♥ MAKE IT YOUR OWN ♥

_____

_____

_____

_____

SUNSHINE LEMON AND LAVENDER SORBET

Yield: 4 servings

Prep time: 25 minutes, plus 1 hour refrigerating time

The perfect refresher for a hot day, this lemony sorbet is made with Meyer lemon juice. Meyer lemons, which taste like a cross between a lemon and a tangerine, are very aromatic and not as tart as traditional lemons. If you can't find them, replace with regular lemon juice.

¾ c. filtered water

¾ c. orange blossom honey or other light honey

¼ c. orange blossom water

1 tbsp. fresh lavender flowers, plus more for garnish (optional)

1 c. Meyer lemon juice

Strips of orange peel, for garnish (optional)

Combine the water, honey, and orange blossom water in a small saucepan. Place over very low heat, stirring until all the honey is dissolved. Remove from the heat and stir in the fresh lavender flowers. Let steep until cool.

Strain out the flowers and stir in the lemon juice. Transfer the mixture to a bowl and place in the refrigerator for about 1 hour, or until well chilled.

Pour the sorbet mixture into an ice-cream maker. Churn for 20 minutes, or until thick. (Alternatively, pour the sorbet mixture into a freezable container and freeze until firm, 2–4 hours.) If desired, garnish with orange peel and lavender flowers. Serve immediately or store in the freezer.

♥ MAKE IT YOUR OWN ♥

MANGO BASIL SORBET

Yield: 4 servings

Prep time: 30 minutes, plus 1 hour refrigerating time

1 lemon grass stalk, white part only, chopped

½ c. filtered water

½ c. raw honey

½ c. fresh basil leaves

2 mangoes

Juice of 1 lime

Thai food is my all-time favorite food to prepare and eat! I simply love the balance of flavors ranging from sweet to spicy, as well as the abundance of color and nutrients that go into each dish. The aromas are out of this world, sensuous from the fresh scent of lemon grass to the zing of galangal. You can't help but feel invigorated by these tropical aromas. There is a charming Thai restaurant overlooking the canals in Venice (California) that I frequent, and every time I'm there I feel like moving to Thailand. That's not to be, but I can still make use of the wonderful Thai flavors—just as this tasty sorbet does.

Combine the lemon grass, water, and honey in a small saucepan. Place over very low heat, stirring until the honey is dissolved. Add the basil and let mixture cool to room temperature.

Peel and chop the mangoes. Place in a blender and add the cooled honey mixture and lime juice. Blend until smooth. Place in the refrigerator for about 1 hour, or until well chilled.

Pour the sorbet mixture into an ice-cream maker. Churn for 20 minutes, or until thick. (Alternatively, pour the sorbet mixture into a freezable container and freeze until firm, 2–4 hours.) Serve immediately or store in the freezer.

♥ MAKE IT YOUR OWN ♥

CARROT MANGO ALMOND SORBET

Yield: 8 servings

Prep time: 10 minutes, plus 2–4 hours freezing time

What makes this sorbet unique, aside from its strikingly vibrant color, is the hint of almond flavor that pops out of the sweet layers of fruit. I've always found this to be an adult crowd-pleaser—as well as a great way to sneak good-for-you fruits and veggies into kids' desserts.

3 medium carrots

2½ c. frozen mango chunks

1 tsp. peeled and chopped fresh ginger

1 c. almond milk

2 tbsp. raw honey (optional)

1 tsp. vanilla extract

½ tsp. almond extract

Peel the carrots, chop into quarters, and place in a food processor. Process until the pulp is evenly chopped (you are looking for a fluffy texture that's not too runny). You should have about 2 c. carrot pulp.

Place the carrot pulp, mango, ginger, almond milk, honey (if desired), vanilla extract, and almond extract in a blender and blend until smooth. Transfer to a freezer-safe container and freeze until the mixture reaches the desired firmness, 2–4 hours. Serve immediately or store in the freezer.

♥ MAKE IT YOUR OWN ♥

SIX

CANDY AND OTHER SWEET BITES

TRAIL-BLAZING TRUFFLES

Yield: 35 truffles
Prep time: 40 minutes

NOUGAT

1 c. pecans
½ c. cashews
½ tsp. vanilla bean powder or vanilla extract
¼ c. agave nectar

CHOCOLATE COATING

¼ c. coconut crystals
½ c. plus 1 tbsp. cacao powder
¾ c. plus 2 tbsp. melted cacao butter (see page 27)
2 tbsp. almond butter

OPTIONAL TOPPINGS

2 tbsp. pistachio pieces
2 tbsp. goji berries
2 tbsp. hemp seeds
2 tbsp. cacao nibs

When my career as a dessert maker was in its beginnings, this was one of the first of my sweets that I shared with friends, family, and clients. These truffles require a lot of hands-on work, which really infuses them with love—the reason they make the perfect gift. Opening a box of handmade chocolates brings so much joy to the recipient (and if he or she shares, everyone in the room). Use an assortment of toppings and the truffles look particularly beautiful.

Line a tray with parchment paper.

To make the nougat: Place the pecans and cashews in a food processor and process until finely broken down. Add the vanilla bean powder and agave nectar and process again until the mixture forms a ball. Do not overprocess or the mixture will become mushy.

Pinch off small amounts of the mixture and roll between your palms to form balls the size of a marble. Set the nougat balls on the tray and place in the refrigerator until ready to use. Make the chocolate coating.

To make the chocolate coating: Using a coffee or spice grinder, grind the coconut crystals into a very fine powder. In a small bowl, combine the cacao powder, coconut crystals, melted cacao butter, and almond butter. Mix well.

To assemble: Remove the nougat balls from the refrigerator and, using a fork, one by one dip them into the chocolate, then place on a piece of parchment paper. Once the chocolate has dried a bit (you can tell it's dry when it turns matte) dip again and sprinkle the toppings onto the wet chocolate coating, if desired. Place the truffles in the refrigerator until the chocolate has hardened completely. Serve immediately or store in the freezer.

♥ MAKE IT YOUR OWN ♥

CHOCOLATE-COVERED TURTLES

Yield: 8 turtles

Prep time: 20 minutes, plus about 15 minutes for turtles to set

CHOCOLATE COATING

1 c. cacao powder

1 c. melted cacao butter (see page 27)

¼ c. agave nectar

CARAMEL

6 large pitted dates

2 tsp. lucuma powder

1 tsp. vanilla extract

1 c. chopped pecan pieces or halves

I love making candy, but I hate using candy thermometers! All that waiting and wondering if you're getting the mixture to the right temperature. That's not a problem here. The only heat you need to use is for melting the cacao butter, and there's no thermometer involved.

To make the chocolate coating: In a small bowl, combine the cacao powder, melted cacao butter, and agave nectar and whisk until smooth. Transfer to a squirt bottle and set the bottle in a warm spot until ready to use. (If you do not have a squirt bottle, leave in the bowl.) Make the caramel.

To make the caramel: Place the dates, lucuma powder, and vanilla extract in a food processor and process until a ball forms. Set aside. (This will stay soft and pliable if left out on the counter for a couple of hours uncovered.)

To assemble: Line a rimmed baking sheet with parchment paper. Squirt the chocolate onto the parchment to form eight 1″ rounds. If you don't have a squirt bottle, use a spoon to create the rounds. Place the rounds in the freezer for 15 minutes or until the chocolate has a matte look, signaling that it's completely dry.

Pinch off quarter-size pieces of the caramel with your fingers, then press a little on top of each chocolate round to create a second layer. Press a pecan half or a few chopped pecans on top of each. Squirt or spoon the remaining chocolate over the turtles, covering the entire round. Return to the refrigerator until the chocolate hardens. Store leftover turtles in the freezer.

DARK CHOCOLATE ALMOND BARK WITH SEA SALT

Yield: One 9x13" bark
Prep time: 10 minutes, plus 15 minutes freezing time

1 c. melted cacao butter
(see page 27)

1¼ c. cacao powder

1 tsp. coarse sea salt

⅓ c. agave nectar

1½ tsp. almond extract

1 tsp. vanilla extract

½ c. almond pieces

Nothing could be as simple yet as impressive as this almond bark. Wrapped in parchment paper and tied with candy cane-striped string, it makes a lovely holiday gift.

Line a 9x13" baking sheet with parchment paper or plastic wrap, allowing the paper or wrap to hang over the sides.

Place the melted cacao butter in a medium bowl and stir in the cacao powder, sea salt, agave nectar, almond extract, and vanilla extract. Mix until smooth. Pour the mixture into the lined pan and sprinkle the almond pieces throughout the pan. Place in the freezer until firm, about 15 minutes. Break the bark apart and store the remaining pieces in the freezer for up to 1 month.

♥ MAKE IT YOUR OWN ♥

FRESH MINT CHOCOLATE HEARTS

Yield: 48 small hearts
Prep time: 10 minutes, plus 20 minutes freezing time

1 c. cacao powder

1 c. melted cacao butter (see page 27)

¼ c. agave nectar

1¼ tsp. mint extract

¾ c. fresh mint leaves, for garnish

I use heart-shaped molds to make these delectable candies. Molds can be purchased from a candy supply store, cookware store, or online. I use mini hearts—perfect for portion control—however, larger molds will do just as well. You'll just end up with fewer hearts. If you don't have molds, see the instructions for using a heart-shaped cookie cutter, below.

Place the cacao powder, melted cacao butter, agave nectar, and mint extract in a medium bowl and whisk until smooth. Pour into heart molds or cookie cutters.* Garnish each chocolate heart by pressing a mint leaf into the top. Place in the freezer until set, approximately 20 minutes. Flip the mold over onto a clean surface and remove the chocolate hearts. Arrange on a plate and serve or store in the freezer.

* If you don't have heart molds, use a small heart cookie cutter. Instead of pouring the chocolate into the molds, line a shallow 11x8" rectangular dish with parchment paper. Pour the chocolate into the dish and place in the refrigerator until slightly firm but still soft enough that pressing a cookie cutter into the chocolate leaves an impression, about 10 minutes. Using the cookie cutter, stamp 48 hearts. Remove the chocolate scraps (as you would when making cookies) and continue as directed.

♥ MAKE IT YOUR OWN ♥

GREEN TEA CHOCOLATE BRITTLE

Yield: Approximately 8 pieces
Prep time: 10 minutes, plus about 30 minutes freezing time

Unlike traditional nutty brittle, where the nuts are used whole or halved, this recipe calls for ground macadamia nuts, so the candy has a smooth texture. What also makes this brittle unusual is the addition of matcha powder. Although there's only a touch of it here, I try to add antioxidants to my desserts whenever possible.

½ c. macadamia nuts

1 tsp. matcha powder

½ c. melted cacao butter (see page 27)

¼ c. agave nectar

1 tsp. vanilla extract

Line a 4x4″ baking pan with parchment paper. Set aside.

Using a food processor, blender, or grinder, process the macadamia nuts to a flourlike consistency.

Place the ground macadamia nuts, matcha powder, melted cacao butter, agave nectar, and vanilla extract in a food processor or high-speed blender and process until smooth. Using a rubber spatula, scrape the mixture onto the parchment paper and spread evenly across the pan. Freeze until solid, about 30 minutes, then break apart with your hands into palm-size pieces. Store in the freezer.

♥ MAKE IT YOUR OWN ♥

_____

_____

_____

_____

CRUNCHY PEANUT BUTTER CUPS

Yield: 12 cups
Prep time: 10 minutes, plus about 30 minutes freezing time

¼ c. cacao butter

2 tbsp. coconut butter

¼ c. cacao powder

2 tbsp. maple syrup

⅓ c. creamy peanut butter, at room temperature

2 tbsp. cacao nibs, for garnish

If, like me, you grew up with Reese's Peanut Butter Cups, these will give you a nice dose of nostalgia. As a kid, I would try different ways of nibbling away at the two-to-a-pack cups. I'd generally eat one in the traditional fashion, then try to hollow out the center of the other one or peck away at the chocolate until mostly peanut butter was left. Now that I'm a grown-up, I've found a better outlet for my, um, creativity. It involves taking the basic recipe for these peanut butter cups and mixing it up. Sometimes, for instance, I'll make them with almond or hazelnut butter instead of peanut butter, or stir in crunchy extras like cacao nibs and hemp seeds. Tossing in some dried fruit can be delicious, too. To make a yummy topping for ice cream or cake, crumble some of these cups into a jar in your freezer.

Set 12 petit cupcake liners on a plate.

Place the two butters in the top of a double boiler and melt over low heat. If you do not have a double boiler, place the butters in a medium heatproof bowl over a small pot of simmering water. Stir the butters as they melt.

Add the cacao powder and maple syrup to the pot or bowl and whisk until smooth.

Transfer the chocolate mixture to a squeeze bottle, or prepare to use a funnel. Squirt (or spoon through the funnel) chocolate into the base of the cupcake liners, filling them one-third

---

♥ TIPS & TRICKS ♥

Besides switching up the type of nut butter you use to make these cups, you can also make them double-decker. Simply use a larger cupcake liner and after you add the second layer of chocolate, spread another layer of nut butter on top. Cover with more chocolate and top with the cacao nibs. You'll need to double the amount of nut butter and chocolate called for to make the double-deckers.

of the way. Swirl the chocolate around the edges of the liner, then place the plate in the freezer until the chocolate sets, about 10 minutes.

Spoon peanut butter over the chocolate, filling the cupcake liners another third of the way. Tap the liners on the counter to remove any air bubbles. Cover the peanut butter layer with another layer of chocolate, then sprinkle cacao nibs on top. Place in the freezer until the chocolate sets completely, about 30 minutes. Serve immediately or store in the freezer.

♥ **SAVOR THIS** ♥

Peanuts are neither a nut nor a pea—they actually belong to the legume family. Unlike nuts, which grow on trees, peanuts start growing on the ground, then burrow underground as they mature. Peanuts are high in protein and rich in healthy fat. They can be eaten raw, but most varieties on the market are roasted. If you can't find raw peanuts, consider the alternative, jungle peanuts.

♥ **MAKE IT YOUR OWN** ♥

NUT BUTTER FREEZER FUDGE

Yield: 12 pieces
Prep time: 20 minutes, plus about 30 minutes freezing time

2 tbsp. melted coconut butter

2 tbsp. coconut oil

½ c. peanut butter or nut or seed butter of your choice

¼ c. coconut nectar

2 tbsp. cacao powder

1 tsp. vanilla bean powder or vanilla extract

¼ tsp. fine sea salt

At the Original Farmers Market in Los Angeles, a wonderful assemblage of shops and eateries that's been around since 1934, you can watch candy makers prepare fudge on big slabs of marble. It can make you want to run home and do the same—only who has five feet of marble? Not to worry if you don't. This yummy fudge is easily made on a rimmed baking sheet. Perhaps not as romantic as marble, but once you're eating the fudge you'll forget all about that. I make it with peanut butter, but you can use any nut butter you like.

Line an 11x8″ rimmed baking sheet with parchment paper.

Place the melted coconut butter in the bowl of a stand mixer or, if using a hand mixer, a medium bowl. Add the coconut oil, peanut butter, coconut nectar, cacao powder, vanilla bean powder, and sea salt and beat until smooth. Using a rubber spatula, scrape the mixture onto the parchment paper and spread evenly across the pan. Using cookie cutters, press shapes lightly into the fudge, or cut into squares. Freeze until firm, about 30 minutes. Serve immediately or store in the freezer.

♥ MAKE IT YOUR OWN ♥

_____

_____

_____

_____

MARZIPAN

Yield: Approximately ½ cup
Prep time: 5 minutes, plus 10 minutes refrigerating time

Freshly made marzipan beats store-bought every time, especially when you consider how easy it is to make. Leave it plain or color it using one of the natural food colors on page 38. For an even more decadent treat, dip the marzipan in a thin layer of chocolate.

1¼ c. almonds
¼ c. agave nectar
2 tsp. almond extract

Place the almonds, agave nectar, and almond extract in a food processor and process until a ball forms. Remove the ball of marzipan, place it on a plate, and set in the refrigerator for 10 minutes to firm up. Remove from the refrigerator and form into shapes using cookie cutters or mold any way you like. Serve immediately or store in the freezer.

♥ MAKE IT YOUR OWN ♥

_____

_____

_____

_____

CHOCOLATE CHERRY ALMOND ROCA

Yield: 8 bars

Prep time: 25 minutes, plus about 20 minutes refrigerating time

CRUST

12 pitted dates

½ c. coconut flakes

½ tsp. vanilla bean powder or vanilla extract

CREAM

½ c. cashews, soaked and drained (see page 29)

¼ tsp. vanilla bean powder or vanilla extract

2 tbsp. maple syrup

2 tbsp. filtered water

FILLING

1 c. pitted cherries

¼ c. sliced, halved, or whole almonds

CHOCOLATE

¼ c. melted cacao butter (see page 27)

½ c. cacao powder

¼ c. maple syrup

1 tsp. almond extract

Coconut flakes, for garnish (optional)

Almond Roca, in its familiar carnation-colored canister, is a delight. This healthier version captures its sweet, toffee-almond essence, but does so with a completely different (and more nutritious) group of ingredients.

Line a 6x6″ baking pan with parchment paper.

To make the crust: Combine the dates, coconut flakes, and vanilla bean powder in a food processor and process until the mixture sticks together when pressed between your fingers. Press the crust into the parchment-lined pan. Set aside and make the cream.

To make the cream: Place the cashews, vanilla bean powder, maple syrup, and water in a blender or food processor and blend until smooth. Spread the cream evenly over the crust. Set aside and make the filling.

To make the filling: Scatter the cherries evenly across the cream. Sprinkle the almonds on top. Place the pan in the refrigerator while making the chocolate.

To make the chocolate: Place the melted cacao butter in a small bowl or glass measuring cup and add the cacao powder, maple syrup, and almond extract. Stir until smooth.

To finish: Pour a layer of chocolate over the entire dessert and set in the refrigerator for 20 minutes or until hardened. Cut into bars and, if desired, garnish with coconut flakes. Serve immediately or store in the freezer.

♥ MAKE IT YOUR OWN ♥

"SNICKERS" BARS

Yield: 12 bars
Prep time: 20 minutes, plus 20 minutes freezing time

CHOCOLATE

2 c. cacao powder

**1 tsp. vanilla bean powder
or vanilla extract**

**1 c. melted cacao butter
(see page 27)**

½ c. coconut nectar

**1 tbsp. melted coconut oil
(see page 28)**

CARAMEL NOUGAT

15 pitted dates

2 tbsp. filtered water

1 tsp. butterscotch extract

1 tsp. vanilla extract

¼ c. almonds or jungle peanuts

If you're a fan of chewy, nutty, chocolaty candy (and who isn't?), you'll enjoy this variation on the Snickers bar. You can use any date you like to make these bars; just bear in mind that the softer the date the easier it is to break down, and that honey and khadrawi dates, in particular, have a very caramel-like flavor.

Line a 9x13" baking pan with parchment paper.

To make the chocolate: Place the cacao powder, vanilla bean powder, melted cacao butter, coconut nectar, and melted coconut oil in a small bowl and stir with a spoon until smooth with no clumps. Pour half of the chocolate into the parchment-lined baking pan, creating a layer no thicker than ¼". Place the bowl with the remaining chocolate in a warm place on your counter. Set the pan with the chocolate layer in the freezer and make the caramel.

To make the caramel nougat: Using a mortar and pestle, food processor, or blender, combine the dates, water, butterscotch extract, and vanilla extract until a paste forms.

To assemble: Remove the pan from the freezer and spread the caramel nougat over the hard chocolate layer. Sprinkle the almonds on top of the caramel and pour the remaining chocolate over the top until the pan is completely filled. Freeze for 15 minutes or until completely hardened.

Remove chocolate from the pan and cut into bars. Serve immediately or store in the freezer.

♥ MAKE IT YOUR OWN ♥

CHOCOLATE-COVERED PRETZELS

Yield: 24 mini pretzels or 4 large
Prep time: 20 minutes, plus about 20 minutes refrigerating time

PRETZEL DOUGH

1 c. sunflower seeds
2 tbsp. flax meal
¼ tsp. sea salt
6 tbsp. raw honey

CHOCOLATE DIPPING SAUCE

¼ c. cacao powder
¼ c. melted cacao butter
(see page 27)
2 tbsp. coconut nectar
¼ tsp. vanilla extract

I'm a sucker for the combination of salty and sweet. These pretzels, made with a dough that contains sunflower seeds, flax meal, and honey and dipped in chocolate, hit the spot.

To make the pretzel dough: Place the sunflower seeds and flax meal in a food processor and process until a fine flour forms. (Do not overprocess or you'll create a butter.) Add the sea salt and while the machine is running add the honey. Stop as soon as the dough forms a ball.

Transfer the dough to a surface lined with parchment paper or a Silpat mat and even out the ball. Cut the dough into quarters. Roll out each quarter of dough into strands ¼" thick by 6" long. Shape each strand into an O, then twist the ends together once. Bring the twisted ends back toward the top of the O and fold it down so the ends lie on top of the curve and the twist is in the middle. Gently press the ends down so they stick to the curve. (See opposite for photos illustrating how to shape pretzels.) Place the pretzels in the refrigerator while making the dipping chocolate.

To make the chocolate dipping sauce: Place the cacao powder, melted cacao butter, coconut nectar, and vanilla extract in a small bowl and whisk to combine.

To assemble: Line a platter or baking sheet with parchment paper. Dip the cold pretzels into the sauce, then gently remove them from the bowl with a fork and place on the parchment paper. Transfer the pretzels to the refrigerator until the chocolate hardens, approximately 10 minutes. Dip again and refrigerate until the second coat of chocolate is completely dry. Serve immediately or store in an airtight container in the refrigerator.

♥ MAKE IT YOUR OWN ♥

_____

_____

_____

_____

MAPLE COCONUT CASHEW BUTTER

Yield: About 1 cup
Prep time: 10 minutes

1½ c. whole cashews

3 tbsp. coconut flakes

½ tsp. ground cinnamon

**¼ tsp. vanilla bean powder
or vanilla extract**

7 tsp. maple syrup

**2 tsp. melted coconut oil
(see page 28)**

If you've perused the nut butter section of your local market lately you may have noticed that the manufacturers have gotten very creative—the number of flavors out there now is wonderful. But it's also simple to make an interesting nut butter of your own; just add your favorite flavorings and you're in business. This Maple Coconut Cashew Butter can serve as a template for your own creations. Or just stick to the recipe. You'll be rewarded with a butter that's delish enough to eat out of the jar.

Place the cashews in a food processor and process until a butter forms, 5–7 minutes.

Once creamy, add the coconut flakes, cinnamon, vanilla bean powder, maple syrup, and melted coconut oil and process until smooth. Store in a jar in a cool, dry place or in the refrigerator.

♥ MAKE IT YOUR OWN ♥

_____

_____

_____

_____

SEVEN

SHAKES AND SIPS

DULCE DE LECHE SHAKE

Yield: 1 serving
Prep time: 15 minutes

You don't need to have ice cream to make a shake. Here, coconut meat acts as a thickener instead and the effect is just as smooth and creamy.

Place the coconut meat, banana, ice cubes, almond milk, vanilla extract, and butterscotch extract in a blender and blend until smooth. Drizzle 1 tbsp. of the caramel into a tall, empty chilled glass, drizzling it down the sides. Pour the shake into the glass and drizzle the remaining 1 tbsp. caramel on top. Serve immediately.

1 c. frozen coconut meat (1–1½ coconuts)

½ large banana, peeled and frozen

6 ice cubes

½ c. almond milk

2 tsp. vanilla extract

½ tsp. butterscotch extract

2 tbsp. caramel sauce (page 34)

♥ MAKE IT YOUR OWN ♥

_____

_____

_____

_____

♥ TIPS & TRICKS ♥

Scoop the meat out of fresh coconuts and freeze it for later! By doing so, you'll find that you always have a great shake or smoothie base handy.

CUTIE CREAMSICLE SHAKE

Yield: 2 servings
Prep time: 8 minutes

5 Satsuma mandarins or other tangerines, peeled and separated into wedges (reserve 2 wedges for garnish)

1 c. frozen coconut meat (1–1½ coconuts)

6 ice cubes

3 tbsp. coconut crystals

½ tsp. vanilla bean powder or vanilla extract

¼ c. sparkling water

5 tbsp. chilled coconut cream

1 tsp. vanilla extract

½ tsp. orange extract

I love using Satsuma mandarin oranges (a type of tangerine sometimes marketed under the trademark name Cuties) for this shake. They are incredibly easy to peel and, best of all, seedless, allowing you to toss everything in the blender and enjoy that much sooner! For a polished look, use a pastry bag to pipe chilled coconut cream on top for a garnish (though a spoon will do if you don't have a pastry bag).

Place the tangerine wedges, coconut meat, ice cubes, coconut crystals, vanilla bean powder, sparkling water, 3 tbsp. of the coconut cream, vanilla extract, and orange extract in a blender and blend until smooth. Pour into tall, chilled glasses and garnish each with 1 tbsp. of the remaining coconut cream and a tangerine wedge. Serve immediately.

♥ MAKE IT YOUR OWN ♥

SPICE OF LIFE SHAKE

Yield: 2 servings
Prep time: 10 minutes

If you're used to a glass of OJ in the morning, try this spiced citrus and banana shake for a change of pace. It's a lot like life itself: an even balance of sweet and spice, full of flavor, and oh so delightful!

1¼ c. grapefruit juice

6 tbsp. lemon juice

2 bananas, peeled, frozen, and broken into chunks

2 tbsp. peeled and grated ginger

1 tsp. ground cinnamon, plus more for garnish

2 tbsp. honey

1 tsp. vanilla extract

Place the grapefruit and lemon juices in a blender. Add the banana chunks, ginger, cinnamon, honey, and vanilla extract. Blend until smooth. Pour into tall glasses and garnish with a sprinkle of cinnamon. Serve immediately.

♥ MAKE IT YOUR OWN ♥

_____

_____

_____

_____

♥ TIPS & TRICKS ♥

To save time and your knuckles from scraping across the grater (ouch!), store a nugget of peeled ginger in the freezer for super easy grating. The icy flecks of ginger dissolve beautifully over a warm soup or dessert. You'll be happy to apply this trick to your next recipe that calls for grated ginger. You may even find that you incorporate grated ginger into more of your creations now that it's so easy to do.

SCRUBBY J'S PEANUT SHAKE

Yield: 4 servings
Prep time: 10 minutes

1 frozen banana

5 pitted deglet or medjool dates

1 c. frozen blueberries

½ c. fresh coconut meat (about 1 coconut) or yogurt

1 c. almond milk

¼ c. peanut butter or almond butter

1 tsp. vanilla extract

4 tsp. hemp seeds, for garnish

One thing that I give thanks for every day is my home, not so much for the interior, but for the spacious backyard. That's where I plant all my favorite fruits, veggies, herbs, flowers, and trees. Backyard gardening has enriched my life greatly. I receive so much clarity, peace, and wisdom from my garden—and it's a great place to host gatherings, for everything from ice-cream socials to musical jam sessions around the fire pit.

Actually, the friends in my garden come in all forms and include squirrels, raccoons, possums, hummingbirds, butterflies, and a local island scrub-jay family, who I call Scrubby J's for short. It's the Scrubby J's who inspired this shake. One winter, shortly after returning from Costa Rica, where I had tasted the local peanuts, I had an itch to plant some of my own. But before I could even get to it, I discovered the Scrubby J's had planted them for me. I started noticing peanuts popping up in my garden, which made me rack my brain. Had I already planted them? Then one day as I was having breakfast at my picnic table, I spotted two of the J's with peanuts in their mouths. I watched them as they went over to my planter beds and buried them for safekeeping. Mystery solved! This peanut-y shake reminds me once again of what it means to be love fed.

Place the banana, dates, blueberries, coconut meat, almond milk, peanut butter, and vanilla extract in a blender and blend until smooth. Pour into 4 glasses and garnish with 1 tsp. of hemp seeds per glass. Serve immediately.

♥ MAKE IT YOUR OWN ♥

YIN-YANG PROTEIN SHAKES

Yield: 2 servings
Prep time: 15 minutes

1 small banana, sliced

6 pitted deglet noor dates

10 ice cubes

**½ tsp. vanilla bean powder
or vanilla extract**

2 c. almond milk

**¼ c. peanut butter or your
favorite nut butter**

1 tsp. maple extract

**1½ tsp. vanilla protein powder
(optional)**

2 tbsp. cacao powder

1 tbsp. cacao nibs

In Chinese philosophy, yin and yang represent complementary forces. I can't think of two better complementary forces than chocolate and vanilla. This recipe lets you create one glass of vanilla with a dollop of chocolate and one glass of chocolate with a dollop of vanilla. Share it with someone who complements you!

Place the banana, dates, ice cubes, vanilla bean powder, almond milk, peanut butter, maple extract, and, if desired, vanilla protein powder in a blender. Blend until smooth. Pour 1 c. of the shake into a tall glass. Add the cacao powder and cacao nibs to the remaining shake in the blender. Blend until smooth. Divide the chocolate shake between 2 tall glasses. Garnish the vanilla glass and the chocolate glass with a dollop of the other shake to create the yin and yang effect. Serve immediately.

♥ MAKE IT YOUR OWN ♥

PIÑA COOL-ADA SHAKE

Yield: 1 serving
Prep time: 5 minutes

This tropical treat can also serve a crowd. Simply multiply all the ingredients by the number of people you have and blend. The recipe calls for half a banana, but if you like a creamier drink, use a whole one.

1 c. frozen pineapple chunks
½ fresh or frozen banana, sliced
1 c. coconut water
½ tsp. vanilla extract

Place the frozen pineapple, banana, coconut water, and vanilla extract in a blender and blend on high speed. Pour into a tall glass and serve immediately.

♥ MAKE IT YOUR OWN ♥

_____

_____

_____

_____

ANISE FIGGY SHAKE

Yield: 2 servings
Prep time: 10 minutes

1½ c. ice

1½ c. Best Basic Vanilla Ice Cream (page 141)

5 fresh figs, peeled*

1 tsp. vanilla bean powder or vanilla extract

1 c. almond milk

1 tbsp. honey

1 tsp. anise extract

Fresh fig slices, for garnish (optional)

Anise flowers, for garnish (optional)

To peel figs: Remove the stem, cut the fig into fourths, and then using a paring knife separate the skin from the flesh. Discard the skin.

When I eat figs out of hand and even for most desserts, I never peel them. But in a shake, it's much nicer to use just the flesh. Peeling figs is a little tricky, but since you'll just be pureeing the flesh, you don't have to worry if it gets a little smushed in the process.

Place the ice, vanilla ice cream, peeled figs, vanilla bean powder, almond milk, honey, and anise extract in a blender and blend on high speed. Divide between 2 tall glasses. If desired, garnish with fig slices and anise flowers. Serve immediately.

♥ MAKE IT YOUR OWN ♥

VANILLA PINEAPPLE-MANGO BREAKFAST "SOUP"

Yield: 2 servings
Prep time: 10 minutes

I love to eat this soup—kind of like a smoothie in a bowl—for breakfast. Because of the ice-cream base it feels super indulgent, though it's actually very nourishing. Of course, it makes a lovely dessert or snack, too. I call for my homemade vanilla ice cream in this recipe, but of course you can use any type of store-bought vanilla ice cream, too.

1 c. frozen pineapple chunks

½ c. frozen mango chunks

½ c. **Best Basic Vanilla Ice Cream (page 141)**

4 pitted medjool dates

2 tbsp. peeled and grated ginger

1 c. freshly made Basic Sweetened Nut Milk (page 31) or store-bought unsweetened vanilla almond milk

Mango slices, for garnish (optional)

Pumpkin seeds, for garnish (optional)

Goji berries, for garnish (optional)

Place the pineapple, mango, ice cream, dates, ginger, and nut milk in a blender. Blend on high speed until smooth. Divide between 2 bowls. If desired, garnish with fresh mango slices, pumpkin seeds, and goji berries. Serve immediately.

♥ MAKE IT YOUR OWN ♥

MANGO LASSI

Yield: 2 servings
Prep time: 10 minutes

1 ripe mango, peeled, pitted, and chopped

1 c. ice

1 c. chopped fresh pineapple

4 pitted dates (preferably honey dates)

¼ ripe banana

½ c. vanilla almond milk

Lassis are traditional Indian drinks usually made with yogurt. For a vegan version, I've substituted almond milk and used dates to add sweetness.

Place the mango, ice, pineapple, dates, banana, and vanilla almond milk in a blender and blend on high speed. Divide between 2 tall glasses and serve immediately.

♥ MAKE IT YOUR OWN ♥

LEMON BALM LIMEADE

Yield: 2 servings
Prep time: 10 minutes

Lemon balm, despite its name, isn't lemon at all. It's an herb in the mint family that's long been used to reduce stress, promote sleep, and help with digestion. If you can't find it, lemon will do nicely as a replacement.

1 large fresh coconut, water and meat (enough for about 2 c. liquid and 1 c. meat)

3 limes, peeled and roughly chopped

1 c. fresh lemon balm leaves (or 1 c. peeled, roughly chopped lemon flesh)

1 c. fresh mint leaves

1 tbsp. peeled and roughly chopped ginger

Crack open the coconut to get the water out first; place the water in a bowl. Completely open the coconut and scoop out the meat with a spoon. Roughly chop the coconut meat.

Place the coconut water and meat, chopped limes, lemon balm leaves, fresh mint, and chopped ginger in a juicer or blender. Run the juicer or blend on high speed. If using a blender, strain the mixture through a fine-mesh sieve or a nut milk bag. Serve the limeade chilled over ice in tall glasses.

♥ MAKE IT YOUR OWN ♥

_____

_____

_____

_____

♥ SAVOR THIS ♥

Lemon balm is used medicinally to help aid with relaxation and sleep. It's also an excellent herb for colic, poor digestion, and even vertigo. To reap the benefits of lemon balm, simply make an herbal tea, sometimes called a tisane, from the leaves.

BASIL BERRY KOMBUCHA

Yield: 1 gallon
Prep time: 30 minutes, plus 1 week fermentation time

1 gallon filtered or distilled water

5 oolong tea bags (or black or green tea if you prefer)

1 c. raw sugar

1 scoby*

2 c. store-bought original kombucha**

½ c. raspberries

¼ c. peeled and sliced ginger

1 sprig of basil with a few leaves

*** You can purchase scobys at natural food stores and online.**

***** Once you use your scoby to make kombucha the first time you can omit the store-bought kombucha.**

Kombucha, if you've never tried it, is a naturally effervescent fermented beverage made from tea and something called a scoby. Scoby stands for "symbiotic culture of friendly bacteria and yeast," and it's a type of starter (also called a "mother"), similar to those used to create sourdough bread and vinegar. Kombucha is thought to aid in digestion and strengthen the immune system and, while it may seem like one of those things you might want to leave to the professionals, it's actually very easy to brew at home. In fact, once you get started you won't want to stop.

Clean and dry well a 1-gallon jar. You may also need a second clean, dry 1-gallon jar several days later.

In a large pot, bring the water to a boil. Add the tea bags and stir in the sugar. Once the sugar has dissolved, remove the pot from heat and allow the tea to cool completely to room temperature. Be very mindful of the temperature and patient enough to let it cool completely.

Remove the tea bags from the cooled tea and pour into the gallon jar. Add the scoby, and if the scoby is new, the store-bought kombucha to the jar. (If there is not enough room in the jar for both, remove some of the tea and store it in the refrigerator to create ice tea.) Place a clean dishtowel or two layers of cheesecloth over the mouth of the jar, then seal with a rubber band. Label the jar with a piece of tape so you know what day you began the fermentation process. Set your brew in a warm, dark space and allow it to ferment for 7 days. (You

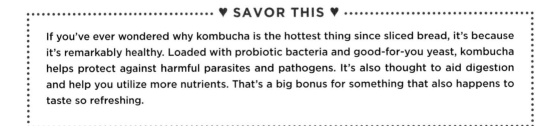

♥ SAVOR THIS ♥

If you've ever wondered why kombucha is the hottest thing since sliced bread, it's because it's remarkably healthy. Loaded with probiotic bacteria and good-for-you yeast, kombucha helps protect against harmful parasites and pathogens. It's also thought to aid digestion and help you utilize more nutrients. That's a big bonus for something that also happens to taste so refreshing.

may decide to let it ferment longer depending on how you'd like it to taste—the longer it sits, the stronger the taste. Begin tasting at 7 days.)

After about 7 days, you will notice a new layer of bacteria and yeast has formed. This is a second scoby, which you can use to start another jar of kombucha or give to friends. Once the kombucha has reached the taste you like, gently remove the scoby with your hands and place it in a bowl. If desired, strain the kombucha into a second clean and dry gallon jar. Add the raspberries, ginger, and basil. Store the kombucha in the refrigerator for up to 5 days.

(I leave the raspberries, ginger, and basil in the kombucha when I know that I will be drinking it within a few days. Otherwise, remove the flavorings after a few days before they spoil.)

If you are retaining the scoby, transfer it back to the original brewing jar and cover it with at least 2" of kombucha. Store in the refrigerator and, when ready, set the jar in a warm, dark spot to continue the fermentation process, then repeat the brewing process again.

♥ MAKE IT YOUR OWN ♥

♥ TIPS & TRICKS ♥

When I posted this recipe on my blog, I received lots of questions. These queries and their answers may help you, too.

Q. My kombucha culture sank to the bottom of my container, is floating sideways, rose to the top of the liquid—in other words, it did different things at different times. Is this normal?
A. Depending on a number of factors (including humidity), the culture may sink, float, or sit sideways. Any of these is normal and will not affect the brewing process.

Q. How long should I brew my kombucha?
A. Seven to 30 days is the range of brewing time and whichever you choose depends on your personal preference. (It can also depend on temperature; kombucha ferments more quickly in warm weather.) A longer brewing time results in a more cultured beverage, but it also makes for a more vinegar-like (less sweet) beverage. Start with 7 days, taste, and proceed as your taste buds tell you to. You can also alter the flavor by adding fruit or juice (at a juice-to-kombucha ratio of about 20:80) following fermentation, which will sweeten the kombucha; adding water to the finished kombucha will dilute it.

Q. I like a very carbonated kombucha. How do I increase the carbonation?
A. After removing the scoby, add juice, fruit, and/or ginger to flavor and allow the kombucha to sit for an additional few days with an airtight lid. This process also allows carbonation to build, so be careful when removing the lid. Keep your whole hand over the lid as you open it.

Q. Can I make kombucha without starter tea?
A. Yes, you can use an equal portion of either distilled white vinegar or pasteurized apple cider vinegar (preferably organic) in place of starter tea. Alternatively, you can purchase bottled kombucha tea at many health food and grocery stores, which can be used. If you choose this option, I recommend using a non-flavored variety of kombucha.

Q. Are there more ways to flavor kombucha?
A. Kombucha can be flavored a zillion different ways. Below are some combinations you might try. Getting the right amounts is a matter of taste. Use the recipe above to give you a general idea of flavor use, then experiment.

Raspberry basil ginger
Lychee ginger
Mint mango blueberry
Strawberry basil
Ginger pear
Peach ginger
Triple berry mint
Kiwi chia

For more information on making kombucha, go to culturesforhealth.com/kombucha-tea -frequently-asked-questions-faq.

WATERMELON PURA FRESCA

Yield: 4 servings
Prep time: 10 minutes

2 c. seeded watermelon cubes
1 c. frozen strawberries, halved
Juice of 2 limes

GARNISHES

4 sprigs of basil
¼ c. coconut flakes
¼ c. goji berries
4 tsp. hemp seeds
8 raspberries

One of the wonderful things about living in Southern California is that you get a taste of Mexico everywhere you go. Many places here sell agua frescas, drinks made with fresh fruit. This recipe puts a twist on watermelon agua fresca by adding several good-for-you non-Mexican garnishes.

Place the watermelon, strawberries, and lime juice in a blender. Blend on high speed until smooth. Pour into 4 glasses and garnish each glass with 1 spring of basil, 1 tbsp. coconut flakes, 1 tbsp. goji berries, 1 tsp. hemp seeds, and 2 raspberries. Serve immediately.

♥ MAKE IT YOUR OWN ♥

PRISTINE GREEN CUCUMBER MINT SIPPING WATER

Yield: 1 quart
Prep time: 5 minutes

I couldn't resist including this refreshing drink in this book. Even though it's not technically a dessert, it's perfect as a snack and beautiful enough to serve to guests (you can even add alcohol if you like). You can choose to give it fizz or not; either way, it's terrifically cleansing and delicious.

In a jar or pitcher, combine the ice, sliced cucumber, green powder, mint leaves, water, lemon juice, lemon soda water (if desired), and agave nectar and stir with a spoon to blend. Serve immediately or store in the refrigerator.

¼ c. ice

¼ c. thinly sliced cucumber

1 tsp. green powder, like Vitamineral Green*

6 fresh mint leaves

1 quart filtered water

Juice of ½ lemon

2 tbsp. lemon soda water (optional)

1 tbsp. agave nectar or sweetener of choice

* Vitamineral Green, a supplement powder full of beneficial minerals from algae and grasses, is popular in the raw food world and often used in shakes. Spirulina, chlorophyll, or wheat grass can be substituted.

························ ♥ MAKE IT YOUR OWN ♥ ··············

_____

_____

_____

_____

····················· ♥ SAVOR THIS ♥ ···················

Having a green powder on hand, such as Vitamineral Green, ensures you'll always have access to green juice even if you don't own a juicer. I especially love traveling with this powder as I know I can always find a fresh glass of juice, such as orange or pineapple, to mix it with for instant feel-good beverage.

HONEY MATCHA LAVENDER LATTE

Yield: 2 servings
Prep time: 12 minutes

1 c. unsweetened vanilla almond milk

1 c. hot filtered water

1 tbsp. matcha powder

4 stems lavender

Pinch of vanilla bean powder or couple drops vanilla extract

1 tsp. orange blossom water

1 tbsp. mango or orange blossom honey (or any raw honey/sweetener you desire)

This is one of the few times in this book that you'll turn on the stove, but all you need is some low heat to make the ingredients blend nicely.

Place the vanilla almond milk and water in a small saucepan and warm over very low heat. Whisk in the matcha powder, lavender, vanilla bean powder, and orange blossom water. Allow the mixture to steep for 10 minutes, and then remove from the heat. Whisk in the honey and strain into glasses.

♥ MAKE IT YOUR OWN ♥

FRUIT—BEYOND BASIC

BERRY PATRIOTIC

Yield: 4 servings
Prep time: 5 minutes

1 c. raspberries
½ c. blackberries
1½ c. blueberries
¼ c. white chia seeds
¼ c. agave nectar
Juice of 1 lemon
Zest of ½ lime

I find the holidays inspiring; celebrations are a great excuse to get into the kitchen and create something new. My goal is generally to develop recipes simple enough to make before rushing off to a party, but still impressive enough to delight my hosts. This red, white, and blue dish (the white comes from the chia seeds) can be made with the berries whole or crushed. It also makes a great spread for breakfast toast.

Place the berries, chia seeds, agave nectar, and lemon juice in a medium serving bowl. Using a rubber spatula or spoon, gently stir so the juices coat all the fruit. Sprinkle the lime zest on top and serve.

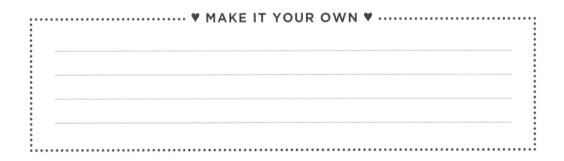

♥ MAKE IT YOUR OWN ♥

RASPBERRY FRUIT FOOL

Yield: 4 servings
Prep time: 10 minutes

FRUIT SWIRL
¾ c. raspberries
¼ c. coconut crystals
Juice of 1 lemon
1 tsp. rose water (optional)

CREAM
2 tbsp. coconut crystals
1¾ c. chilled coconut cream
½ tsp. vanilla bean powder or vanilla extract

This English dessert with the funny/insulting name has existed since the mid-seventeenth century. It's traditionally made with pureed fruit and custard, but I think this coconut cream version is just as delicious. Feel free to substitute kiwis, mango, or any other soft fruit for the berries.

To make the fruit swirl: Place the raspberries, coconut crystals, lemon juice, and, if desired, rose water in a blender and blend until smooth. Strain through a fine-mesh sieve, discard the solids, and set the liquid aside. (You should have just less than 1 c. of raspberry sauce.) Make the cream.

To make the cream: Using a coffee or spice grinder, grind the coconut crystals to a very fine powder. Combine the chilled coconut cream, ground coconut crystals, and vanilla bean powder in a medium bowl or the bowl of an electric mixer. Beat (use a handheld mixer if you don't have a stand mixer) until stiff peaks form.

To assemble: Gently fold the raspberry swirl into the cream, reserving some raspberry swirl for garnish. Spoon into bowls and drizzle the reserved raspberry sauce over the top of the fool. Serve immediately or store in the refrigerator for up to 3 days.

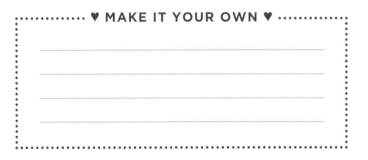

♥ **MAKE IT YOUR OWN** ♥

LAVENDER AND COCONUT CREAM-FILLED STRAWBERRIES

Yield: 12 servings
Prep time: 10 minutes

To make these eye-catching treats, choose the biggest strawberries you can find—that will make them easier to prepare. They are beautiful enough to serve to guests but also make a nice breakfast with a cup of tea, or a midday snack.

12 large strawberries, hulled

2 c. chilled coconut cream

1½ tsp. fresh lavender

¼ tsp. vanilla bean powder or vanilla extract

2 tbsp. raw honey

Cacao nibs, for garnish (optional)

Black chia seeds, for garnish (optional)

Using a paring knife, slightly hollow out the top of the strawberries. Place the strawberries on a platter and set aside.

Pour the coconut cream into a medium bowl. Add the lavender, vanilla bean powder, and honey and whip with a hand mixer on low speed until fluffy.

Place a pastry bag in a tall glass, allowing the edges of the bag to hang over the rim of the glass. Scoop the cream into the bag. (Or use a small offset spatula or small spoon to stuff the strawberries.) Add enough cream to poke out over the tops of the strawberries. Twist your wrist lightly as you finish adding the cream to create a swirl at the top. If desired, garnish the top of the cream with cacao nibs and/or chia seeds. Serve immediately or store in the refrigerator for up to 3 days.

♥ MAKE IT YOUR OWN ♥

FIGS IN LOVE

Yield: 2 servings

Prep time: 20 minutes, plus 1–2 hours for frosting to set

FROSTING

½ c. cashews

½ c. macadamia nuts

1 c. coconut milk

½ c. melted coconut butter

¼ c. agave nectar

1 tbsp. lemon juice

1 tbsp. vanilla extract

4 large figs

16 raspberries

2 tsp. agave nectar

Edible flowers, for garnish
(optional)

You may have noticed: I'm driven by love. (Why else would I call this book Love Fed?*) When I met the man of my dreams, Alex, I began to notice how powerful love can be. I create recipes so effortlessly when I think of Alex; that's how much inspiration he brings to me. This recipe and book are a tribute to the man who brings out my sweet side. It's lovely served with a piece of home-made chocolate on the side.*

To make the frosting: Place the cashews, macadamia nuts, coconut milk, coconut butter, agave nectar, lemon juice, and vanilla extract in a blender and blend until smooth. Pour the mixture into a bowl, cover, and refrigerate until firm, approximately 1–2 hours.

To assemble: Slice a cross pattern three-quarters of the way through the flesh of the figs. Allow the figs to spread open like a flower and place 3 raspberries in the bottom of each. Gently flatten the remaining 4 raspberries with a spoon. Using an ice-cream scoop, add a scoop of frosting on top of the berries. Add a flattened raspberry on top of the frosting and drizzle agave nectar on top. Garnish the plate with edible flowers if desired. Serve immediately or store in the refrigerator for up to 2 days.

♥ MAKE IT YOUR OWN ♥

WATERMELON AND PINEAPPLE SASHIMI

Yield: 2 servings
Prep time: 10 minutes

1 small watermelon
1 small pineapple
1 tbsp. chopped fresh mint leaves
1 tsp. poppy seeds
1 tsp. sesame seeds
Juice of ¼ lime

One early-summer day, I had a gorgeous pineapple and water-melon sitting on my countertop and an urge to amuse myself. I began to think of how I could present these fruits in a new and refreshing way, so I pulled out my veggie peeler and started playing with my food. After one slice into the melon it instantly reminded me of sashimi. The best ideas can come up when your only agenda is to try something new and see what happens.

Cut the watermelon and pineapple into 1″ thick, rind-less wedges. Run a wide vegetable peeler along the front of the wedges to "peel" off thin slices of fruit flesh. (If you don't have a wide vegetable peeler use a sharp knife and cut thin slices.) Gently lay the slices on a plate.

Sprinkle the slices with chopped mint leaves, poppy seeds, sesame seeds, and lime juice. Serve with chopsticks.

♥ MAKE IT YOUR OWN ♥

CITRUS CARPACCIO SUPREME

Yield: 2 servings
Prep time: 10 minutes

1 Valencia orange

1 grapefruit

1 tbsp. pistachios, chopped

1 tsp. orange honey or other honey light in taste and color

¼ tsp. orange blossom water, orange juice, or orange extract

Sometimes a simple orange or grapefruit seems perfect; sometimes they just seem, well, boring. With the addition of just a bit of nuts, honey, and flavoring, this recipe takes citrus from ordinary to extraordinary.

Using a small paring knife, slice off the top and bottom of the orange and grapefruit just enough to expose the pulp. Starting at the top, just where the pith (the white part) meets the pulp, bring your knife downward to slice off the skin of the fruit.

Cut the orange and grapefruit into ¼"-thick round slices and arrange on a platter, alternating colors. Sprinkle with the pistachios, drizzle the orange honey and orange blossom water over the fruit, and serve with chopsticks.

♥ TIPS & TRICKS ♥

The slicing technique I described at left is called supreme. It allows you to gracefully remove the skin, pith, membranes, and seeds. Supreme cutting is also a fabulous way to cut melons and pineapples.

♥ MAKE IT YOUR OWN ♥

FESTIVE SATSUMA CACAO WEDGES

Yield: 6 servings
Prep time: 10 minutes

¼ c. chopped almonds

¼ c. hemp seeds

⅓ c. grated or chopped raw chocolate (page 32)

6 seedless Satsuma tangerines, peeled and sectioned

Keep the ingredients for this dish on hand, and you always have a dessert option at the ready. You can make this in the same time it takes to brew a cup of tea.

Line a plate with parchment paper and chill in the refrigerator.

Place the almonds and hemp seeds on a plate and toss to combine. Set aside.

Place the chocolate in a small saucepan and melt over low heat. Dip the tangerine sections in the chocolate (I like to do a dainty dip, where I only coat the tip). Next dip the chocolate-covered portion of the tangerine sections in the hemp and almonds. Set on the cold parchment-lined dish and place it in the refrigerator for 5 minutes. Serve immediately or store in the refrigerator for up to 3 days.

♥ MAKE IT YOUR OWN ♥

ROSEMARY PECAN CARAMEL APPLES

Yield: 6 small apples or 4 medium
Prep time: 10 minutes, plus 10 minutes for caramel to set

I think of these as grown-up candied apples—that is, they appeal to adults' more sophisticated palate. That said, kids love to eat them, too. They also love to make them and are a great craft project at birthday parties.

6 small or 4 medium Fuji apples, chilled

2 tbsp. lucuma powder

½ c. melted cacao butter (see page 27)

2 tbsp. agave nectar

1 c. chopped pecans

3 tbsp. chopped rosemary

Insert a wooden skewer into the center of the apples.

Place the lucuma powder, cacao butter, and agave nectar in a small bowl and whisk until well combined. Dip the apples in the cacao mixture, covering as much of the apples as possible. Immediately sprinkle with or dip the apple into the pecan pieces. Garnish with rosemary. (Move quickly because the cacao mixture dries fast.) Place the apples, sticks up, on a platter and set in the refrigerator to harden, about 10 minutes. Serve immediately or store in the refrigerator for up to 3 days.

♥ SUBSTITUTIONS ♥

Try making these with other toppings, such as coconut crystals, chia seeds, cacao nibs, and coconut flakes.

♥ MAKE IT YOUR OWN ♥

RESOURCES

Love Fed Staples

What follows is a list of my favorite brands and where to find them. When in doubt, you can always find all the ingredients I use through amazon.com.

COCONUT BUTTER: Artisana Foods is a great source for coconut butter.

artisanafoods.com

COCONUT CREAM: Found at most ethnic markets, including Asian and Indian. Also often available at local grocers. Brands such as Aroy-D and Natural Value are gum-free and BPA-free.

COCONUT OIL AND COCONUT NECTAR: Check out Tropical Traditions.

tropicaltraditions.com

COCONUT PALM SUGAR, CACAO NIBS, HEMP SEEDS, GOJI BERRIES, VANILLA BEAN POW-DER, CACAO POWDER, CACAO BUTTER, MACA, LUCUMA, AND AGAVE: The following companies carry all these ingredients. Most of these companies also sell in bulk, so if you really get into making raw vegan desserts and want to save on cost, buy in bulk.

essentiallivingfoods.com

navitasnaturals.com

sunfood.com

ultimatesuperfoods.com

FAVORITE SOUTHERN CALIFORNIA FARMERS:

Bautista Farms Dates: 7hotdates.com

Harry's Berries: harrysberries.com

Honey Pacifica: honeypacifica.com

ORANGE BLOSSOM WATER AND ROSE WATER: A popular brand sold at common grocery stores is Cortas, which can be purchased through amazon.com.

IRISH MOSS (RAW, WILD-CRAFTED): The Raw Food World is an excellent source for Irish moss and other raw foods.

therawfoodworld.com

NUTS AND SEEDS (CHIA, HEMP, SUNFLOWER): I love using nuts.com. The quality is excellent, the delivery is fast, and it's a family-run business. The nuts are always fresh and the website has a raw section highlighting all of their raw products.

nuts.com

SPECIALTY HONEYS: Honey Pacifica carries my favorite local honeys that are raw and have a wide range of flavor profiles, from buckwheat to mango.

honeypacifica.com

OTHER RESOURCES: I also recommend shopping at a local co-op or health food store that sells items in bulk bins so you can buy what you need and save on manufacturers' packaging. I usually find ingredients such as almond flour, flax meal, nuts, coconut flakes, cacao powder, and dried fruits such as figs and dates in these bulk bins.

INDEX